Life Science Quest
For Middle Grades

By

SCHYRLET CAMERON AND JANIE DOSS

COPYRIGHT © 2008 Mark Twain Media, Inc.

ISBN 978-1-58037-450-7

Printing No. CD-404091

Mark Twain Media, Inc., Publishers
Distributed by Carson-Dellosa Publishing LLC

Visit us at www.carsondellosa.com

Table of Contents

Introduction to the Teacher

Science plays an increasingly important role in every aspect of our lives. Scientific advances have led to many of the comforts we enjoy, as well as the problems our students must solve. The economic productivity of our society has become tightly linked to the scientific skills in the work force. Our future depends on developing a scientifically literate nation that is able to compete on a global scale. It is important that teachers provide students with many opportunities to acquire knowledge, learn skills, explore scientific phenomena, and develop attitudes important to becoming scientifically literate.

This book encourages students to develop an understanding of the concepts and processes of science through the use of good scientific techniques. It supports the National Science Education Standards and is designed to promote scientific inquiry. It can be used to teach the core science curriculum by itself or as supplemental material.

Each unit is designed to encourage students to master basic concepts while building a working scientific vocabulary. The text is arranged in a format that does not overwhelm struggling readers. Visuals, illustrations, diagrams, and charts present information in an easy-to-read format. Key terms appear boldfaced in the text and are followed by the definitions.

Lessons use a variety of effective teaching strategies. Labs permit students to participate in the scientific method: experiment, observe, and infer. Hands-on activities help students understand abstract ideas. Materials used in the activities are commonly found in the classroom. Each activity may be completed in a variety of ways: team experiment, individual student project, or whole-class demonstration. Written projects allow students to practice computer and research skills. Completing graphic organizers helps students retain information and reinforce main ideas. Reviews are designed to evaluate student understanding of key concepts and vocabulary.

Teacher Resource pages present the National Science Education Standards correlated to the unit and give an extensive list of the concepts that will help the teacher organize the lessons. Enrichment activities, interactive websites, and answer keys guide the teacher through each unit.

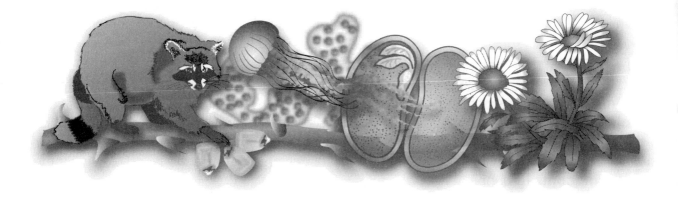

Characteristics of Living Organisms

Characteristics of All Living Things

By observing their **properties** (characteristics that describe an object), scientists have divided all things into two groups: living and non-living. All living things, known as organisms, must have the following characteristics.

Organisms Must:

- be made up of one or more cells.
- need and use energy to carry out life activities.
- use food and excrete waste.
- be **adapted** (suited) to their **environment** (surroundings).
- respond to changes in their environment.
- reproduce organisms like themselves.
- grow and develop.

All Living Things Need:	Why?
Food	- to promote growth and for energy
Water	- to break down other chemicals into tiny particles small enough to go in and out of the cells
Air	- to make and change food into energy
Temperature	- to keep conditions inside their bodies constant
Space	- to get the things they need in order to survive

Classifying Living Things

We could **classify** (organize) living things in many ways: color, size, or shape. A good classification system would be meaningful to those using it, easily understood, and easy to describe to someone else. Two thousand years ago, Aristotle created a classification system that placed all living things in the plant group or animal group. This system did not always work. Scientists continued looking for patterns in the living world in order to find a better system. To eighteenth century scientists Carolus Linnaeus and George Cuvier, it became apparent that living things shared similarities in **anatomy** (structure). Their ideas formed the basis of the modern classification system of kingdom, phylum, class, order, family, genus, and species.

Five Kingdoms

At one time, all organisms were thought to be either plants or animals. The development of the microscope led scientists to the discovery of new living things called **microscopic organisms** (organisms too small to be seen with the unaided eye). As scientists looked closer at these **microbes** (microscopic organisms), they learned that they were not like plants or animals. Based on these new discoveries, scientists decided to divide the world of living things into five **kingdoms** (groups).

Five Kingdoms

Kingdom	Definition	Examples
Monera	- only one kind of organism: bacteria - **unicellular** (made up of only one cell) - without a true nucleus - some are able to move about	*Bacteria*
Protista	- unicellular - some are **protozoa** (animal-like organisms) and move to obtain food - some are **algae** (plant-like organisms) and can make their own food - some are fungus-like and obtain their food from their **hosts** (an animal or plant that nourishes and supports a parasite or another organism)	- paramecium, amoeba, diatom, zooflagellate, chloropyhte *Spirogyra Chloropyhte* *Frustulia Diatom*
Fungi	- **multicellular** (made up of many cells) - cells with a true nucleus - have cell walls - cannot make their own food - cannot move about - absorb energy from their host	- mold, mildew, mushroom, hyphae, lichens *MIldew ascomycete*
Plants	- multicellular - cells with a true nucleus - have cell walls - have chlorophyll - cannot move about - use sunlight to make their food	- ferns, flowers, deciduous trees, coniferous trees *Tulips*
Animals	- cells with a true nucleus - move about in order to eat other organisms	- mammals, birds, amphibians, fish, reptiles, invertebrates *Llama* *Canary*

Cells

Cells, the "building blocks of life," are the smallest living things. All organisms are made up of cells. Some living things are unicellular and carry out all the basic life activities within that single cell. However, most living things are multicellular.

Cell Discoveries

- **Robert Hooke** (1665): The first person to see cells with the aid of an early compound microscope. Hooke looked at a slice of cork and saw small, empty, box-like structures. He thought the box shapes resembled cells, or rooms, monks used for sleeping. He decided to name the structures cells.
- **Anton van Leeuwenhoek** (1674): The first person to observe living cells. He studied pond water and observed single-celled organisms.
- **Matthias Schleiden** (1838): A **botanist** (a person who studies plants) who discovered living plants were made up of cells with nuclei.
- **Theodor Schwann** (1839): A **zoologist** (a person who studies animals) who discovered animals are made up of cells with nuclei.
- **Randolph Virchow** (1855): He believed that an existing cell divided to form new cells.

The early work of scientists such as Robert Hooke and Anton Van Leeuwenhoek, the invention of better microscopes, and new discoveries by scientists in the 1800s led to many new ideas about cells. These ideas were put together as a **theory** (an idea that is repeatedly supported by test results).

Cell Theory

- All organisms are made up of one or many cells.
- Cells are the basic unit of structure and function in all organisms.
- All cells come from other cells that already exist.

Microscope

- A microscope is an important scientific tool.
- Microscopes use **lenses** (curved pieces of glass) and light to magnify very small things in order to make them appear larger.
- There are two kinds of microscopes:
    Simple: contain one lens
    Compound: contain two or more lenses
- The microscopes used in science classrooms are compound microscopes.
- All compound microscopes have the same basic parts.

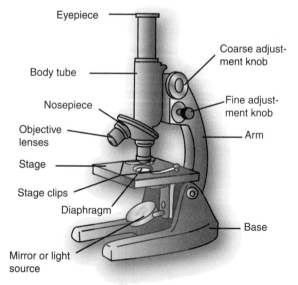

Eyepiece
Coarse adjust-ment knob
Body tube
Fine adjust-ment knob
Nosepiece
Objective lenses
Arm
Stage
Stage clips
Diaphragm
Base
Mirror or light source

Three Main Parts of a Cell

Cells have three things in common. They all have a **nucleus** (control center for the cell), **cell membrane** (a thin layer that encloses the cell), and **cytoplasm** (a gel-like material that contains proteins, nutrients, and all of the other cell organelles).

Nucleus
- controls all the cell activities
- round or egg-shaped structure found near the center of the cell
- dark in color
- contains **DNA** (genetic information)

Cell Membrane
- thin layer that encloses the cell
- controls the movement of material into and out of the cell
- offers shape and protection for the cell

Cytoplasm
- gel-like material
- contains proteins, nutrients, and all of the other **cell organelles** (many tiny structures in cytoplasm, each does a specific job for the cell)

Animal Cell

Plant Cell

Types of Cells: There are two main types of cells.

Cell Type	Definition	Example
Eukaryotic Cell	- cell with nucleus	- most cells - plant and animal cells Animal Cell Plant Cell
Prokaryotic Cell	- cell with no nucleus - DNA and other nuclear materials float "freely" inside the cytoplasm - simplest type of cell	- bacteria and their relatives

Comparing Plant and Animal Cells

All organisms are made up of cells. Some organisms, such as plants and animals, are multicellular. Plant and animal cells have many similarities as well as many differences. Organelles perform a specific **function** (job) for the cell. The organelles help the cell run smoothly and keep it alive.

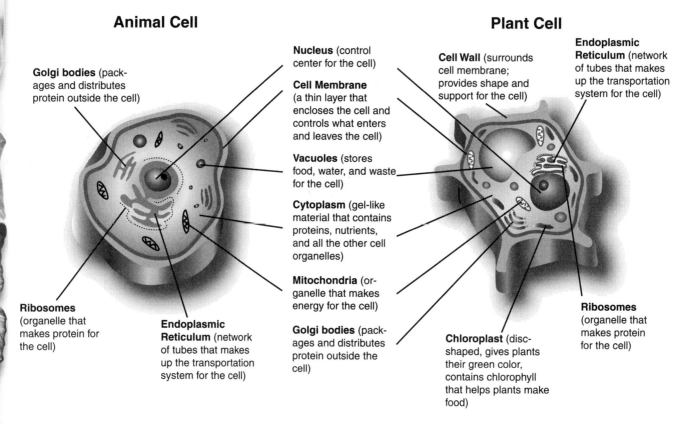

Animal Cell

Plant Cell

Golgi bodies (packages and distributes protein outside the cell)

Nucleus (control center for the cell)

Cell Membrane (a thin layer that encloses the cell and controls what enters and leaves the cell)

Vacuoles (stores food, water, and waste for the cell)

Cytoplasm (gel-like material that contains proteins, nutrients, and all the other cell organelles)

Mitochondria (organelle that makes energy for the cell)

Golgi bodies (packages and distributes protein outside the cell)

Cell Wall (surrounds cell membrane; provides shape and support for the cell)

Endoplasmic Reticulum (network of tubes that makes up the transportation system for the cell)

Ribosomes (organelle that makes protein for the cell)

Endoplasmic Reticulum (network of tubes that makes up the transportation system for the cell)

Chloroplast (disc-shaped, gives plants their green color, contains chlorophyll that helps plants make food)

Ribosomes (organelle that makes protein for the cell)

Cell Diffusion and Osmosis

The cell's membrane controls what enters and leaves a cell. To carry on life processes, oxygen, food, and water must pass through the cell's membrane, and waste products must be removed from the cell through the membrane. The membrane has tiny holes in it. **Molecules** (very small substances) can go in and out by moving through the tiny holes. **Diffusion** (the movement of molecules into and out of the cell) helps the cell carry out all the basic life activities.

Cells contain water and are surrounded by water. A cell needs water to maintain a constant temperature, shape, and size for life processes to occur. **Osmosis** (movement of water molecules into and out of a cell) is a special kind of cell diffusion.

Name: _____ Date: _____

Plant and Animal Cell Lab

Purpose: Compare and contrast plant and animal cells

Materials Needed

onion	slides	cover slips	microscope	needle
water	iodine	eyedroppers	toothpick (flat or blunt)	

Procedure

Plant Cell

Step 1: With the needle, peel the thin clear tissue from the inside section of an onion.
Step 2: Carefully place the tissue flat on a slide. Smooth out any wrinkles in the tissue.
Step 3: Add a drop of iodine to the tissue. View the onion tissue under the microscope, and record your observations below.

Onion Cell

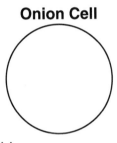

Animal Cell

Step 1: Add a drop of iodine to a slide.
Step 2: Use the blunt end of a toothpick to gently scrape the inside lining of your cheek. Place the blunt end of the toothpick on the slide and mix it with the iodine.
Step 3: Place a cover slip over the mixture. View the slide under the microscope, and record your observations below.

Cheek Cell

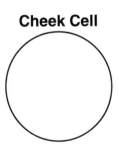

Conclusion

What similarities and differences did you observe when viewing the plant and animal cells under the microscope?

_____

_____

_____

_____

Name: _____ Date: _____

Plant and Animal Cell Venn Diagram

1. Compare and contrast plant and animal cells using a Venn diagram.

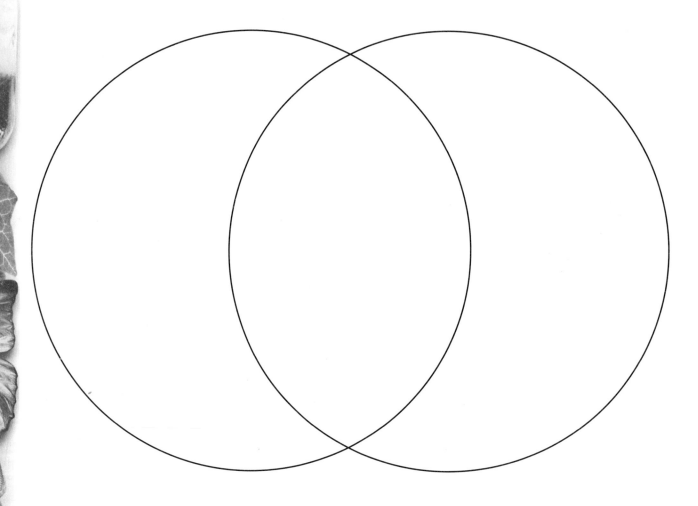

2. Why do plant cells have a cell wall and animal cells do not?

_____

_____

_____

_____

Name: _____ Date: _____

Gelatin Cell Model

Purpose: To compare plant and animal cells

Materials Needed

plastic sandwich bags
raisins
For each batch:
2 $\frac{1}{2}$ cups boiling water

half-pint milk cartons (with tops removed)
celery, cubed

4 packages lemon gelatin

Procedure

Day 1
    Step 1: Line the milk carton with the sandwich bag, allowing the excess part of the bag to extend over the edges of the milk carton.
    Step 2: Stir gelatin into boiling water until dissolved.
    Step 3: When the gelatin has cooled but not gelled, pour $\frac{1}{4}$ cup into each lined carton.
    Step 4: When the mixture begins to gel, have all students gently push a raisin (nucleus) into the gelatin. Give half the students several celery cubes (chloroplast) to add to their gelatin. Refrigerate overnight.

Day 2
    Step 1: Prepare a second batch of gelatin mixture. Slowly add ¼ cup of the mixture to each milk carton.
    Step 2: Once the mixture has completely cooled, close the sandwich bag.
    Step 3: Refrigerate the cartons of gelatin until the gelatin is firm.
    Step 4: Students with celery in the mixture leave their sandwich bags in the carton. Students without celery take their sandwich bags out of the carton.

Conclusion

Which model represents an animal cell and which represents a plant cell? Explain your answer.

_____

_____

_____

_____

Name: _____ Date: _____

Osmosis Lab

Purpose: Demonstrate the process of osmosis in plants

Materials Needed

1 packet unflavored gelatin

sandwich bags

½ cup iodine

measuring cups

½ cup water

perfume

glass beaker or jar

Procedure

Step 1: Stir the gelatin into one cup of boiling water until dissolved.

Step 2: Add cold water and a few drops of perfume.

Step 3: Pour mixture into a sandwich bag, seal, and refrigerate until solid.

Step 4: Add warm water and iodine to the glass beaker or jar.

Step 5: Place the sandwich bags of solid gelatin into the glass beaker or jar.

Observation

1. After a few hours, look at the bag. Record your observation.

   _____

   _____

   _____

   _____

2. Smell the water in the jar. Record your observations.

   _____

   _____

   _____

   _____

Apply

Explain how this experiment demonstrates the process of osmosis.

_____

_____

_____

_____

Name: _____   Date: _____

Cell Review

Part I

Directions: Write the letter of the correct answer on the line.

_____ 1. All living things are made up of _____.
   a. only one cell   b. one or more cells   c. many cells   d. tissues

_____ 2. Substances move in and out of the cell by a process called _____.
   a. osmosis   b. diffusion   c. respiration   d. photosynthesis

_____ 3. Cells with a true membrane-bound nucleus are called _____.
   a. eukaryotic   b. prokaryotic   c. organelles   d. plant

_____ 4. _____ are structures within the cell.
   a. Cell walls   b. Cell membranes   c. Organelles   d. Osmosis

_____ 5. All organisms need _____ to promote growth and for energy.
   a. water   b. food   c. air   d. space

Part II

Directions: Name the three main parts of a cell. Write the answers on the lines.

1. _____
2. _____
3. _____

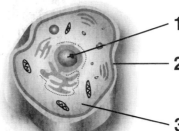 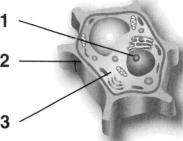

Part III

Directions: Complete the chart by listing the function of each cell part.

Cell Part	Function
nucleus	
cell membrane	
cytoplasm	
chloroplast	
cell wall	

DNA

Scientists studied cells for many years before they discovered how **traits** (characteristics) of the parents were passed on to their offspring. By the end of the nineteenth century, scientists had learned the secret code of **heredity** (passing physical and character traits from one generation to another). **Chromosomes** (rod-shaped strands containing genetic material) located in the nucleus of the cell are made up of genes. The genes consisted of a long strand of DNA. The DNA contains the **genetic blueprint** (code) for how an organism looks and functions. The substances in the DNA are arranged in a three-dimensional structure that looks like a ladder. During cell division, the ladder unzips and gives each new cell a copy of the genetic information.

DNA Discoveries

- **Gregor Mendel** (1857): described how traits called genes are inherited
- **Frederick Griffith** (1928): proved the existence of an inheritance molecule
- **Oswald Avery** (1944): identified DNA as the inheritance molecule
- **Rosalind Franklin** (1951): discovered the double-helix shape of DNA
- **Francis Crick** and **James Watson** (1953): constructed a model of the DNA molecule

Making a DNA Model

A single DNA molecule, or ladder, can have thousands of rungs, or steps. The number of steps and how they are arranged form a genetic code. The genetic code determines the different kinds of inherited traits.

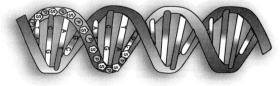

Materials Needed

6 different colors of beads   pipe cleaners

Directions

Use the information below to construct a DNA model. String beads on pipe cleaners to represent a pattern of phosphates (P); deoxyribose (D), a kind of sugar; and the four nitrogen bases present in DNA: adenine (A), cytosine (C), guanine (G), and thymine (T). Twist the pipe cleaners together to form the sides and rungs of a miniature DNA ladder.

1. Each side of the ladder is made up of alternating units of phosphates and deoxyribose.
   Side 1: P-D-P-D-P-D-P-D-P-D-P-D-P-D-P-D-P-D-P-D-P-D-P-D-
   Side 1: P-D-P-D-P-D-P-D-P-D-P-D-P-D-P-D-P-D-P-D-P-D-P-D-

2. The 4 bases form the rungs or steps on the ladder. The bases will only pair up with each other in a certain manner. Adenine pairs only with thymine and cytosine only pairs with guanine.
   Side 1: P-D-P-D-P-D-P-D-P-D-P-D-P-D-P-D-P-D-P-D-P-D-P-D-
             A   T   C   G   A   G   T   C   A   T   C
             T   A   G   C   T   C   A   G   T   A   G
   Side 1: P-D-P-D-P-D-P-D-P-D-P-D-P-D-P-D-P-D-P-D-P-D-P-D-

Name: _____ Date: _____

DNA Lab

Purpose: Observe onion cell DNA

Materials Needed

1 cup chopped onion	$\frac{1}{4}$ cup warm water	blender	funnel
1 teaspoon salt	$\frac{1}{4}$ cup liquid dish soap	toothpicks	slides
2 small beakers or jars	meat tenderizer	microscope	

Procedure

Step 1: Blend chopped onions, warm water, and salt.

Step 2: Pour mixture into a small glass beaker or jar.

Step 3: Add liquid dish soap and mix gently for 5 minutes.

Step 4: Pour mixture into the funnel and filter out all the liquid into another small glass beaker or jar.

Step 5: Add meat tenderizer to the liquid.

Step 6: Measure the filtered liquid.

Step 7: Add an equal amount of rubbing alcohol to the mixture. The alcohol will form a separate layer on top of the onion mixture.

Step 8: The white strings floating to the top are DNA. Gently stir the alcohol layer.

Step 9: Use a toothpick to remove a white DNA string and place on a slide.

Observation

Observe the DNA under a microscope. Record your observations.

_____

_____

_____

_____

Apply

If you removed DNA from other plants, would it look different from the DNA of an onion? Explain your answer.

_____

_____

_____

_____

Mitosis

All living things grow and repair themselves by the process of **mitosis** (the process of cell division). To make a cell, everything inside the cell must first be copied. The cell contents and DNA are divided equally between two **daughter cells** (new cells). There are five steps in mitosis.

Normal Cell	Step 1: Interphase	Step 2: Prophase	Step 3: Metaphase
	- DNA breaks up into short chromosomes - each chromosome makes an exact copy of itself - each pair of chromosomes stays attached at the **centromere** (middle)	- chromosomes become visible - nuclear membrane disappears - threadlike spindle fibers stretch across the cells	- chromosomes line up randomly along the middle of the cell - each chromosome's centromere attaches to a spindle fiber

Step 4: Anaphase	Step 5: Telophase	Cytokinesis
- spindle fibers pull each pair of chromosomes apart and toward opposite ends of the cell	- nuclear membrane begins to form around the two sets of duplicated chromosomes - the cell pinches apart in the middle	- divided cell forms two daughter cells

Meiosis

Meiosis (the two-step process of sex-cell formation) produces **gametes** (reproductive cells: egg and sperm). Gametes contain only half the normal number of chromosomes as normal cells. Meiosis I has the same steps and names as those in mitosis.

Meiosis I

Normal Cell	Step 1: Interphase	Step 2: Prophase	Step 3: Metaphase

Step 4: Anaphase	Step 5: Telophase	Cytokinesis

Meiosis II

- daughter cells go through a second division of the nucleus - no chromosome replication	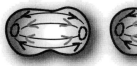 

Gametes formed	
- chromosome pairs are split apart - four **genomes** (daughter cells with half the number of chromosomes) are formed	

During fertilization, reproductive cells unite; the full number of chromosomes for the formation of normal cells is restored. The cell then has traits or genetic material from both parents.

Name: _____ Date: _____

Mitosis and Meiosis Models

Purpose: Illustrate the steps in cell division during mitosis and meiosis

Materials Needed

assortment of colored pipe cleaners
yarn
glue

paper plates
hole puncher

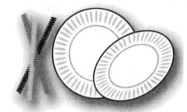

Procedure

Step 1: Use paper plates to represent the steps a cell goes through during mitosis.
Step 2: Label each plate with the phase it represents.
Step 3: Use different colored pipe cleaners to represent the chromosomes and pieces of yarn to represent the thread-like spindle fibers. Arrange and glue the materials on the plates to illustrate the phases of mitosis.
Step 4: Punch a hole on each side of the plates. Using yarn, attach the plates to form a long train.
Step 5: Construct a model of meiosis following steps 1, 2, and 3 using paper plates, pipe cleaners, and yarn.

Apply

Compare and contrast the processes of mitosis and meiosis.

_____

_____

_____

_____

_____

_____

Mitosis and Meiosis Poster

Create a poster illustrating the steps in mitosis or meiosis. Label and describe each step.

Name: _____ Date: _____

Cell Division Review

Part I
Directions: Match the definition with the correct vocabulary word.

_____ 1. mitosis

_____ 2. gametes

_____ 3. DNA

_____ 4. traits

_____ 5. meiosis

a. genetic blueprint for cell

b. characteristics

c. process of sex cell formation

d. produces cells for growth and repair

e. sperm and egg cells

Part II
Direction: Label the steps in mitosis.

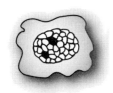 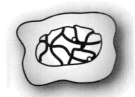 

1. _____   2. _____   3. _____

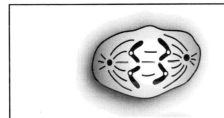 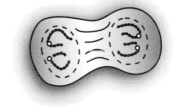

4. _____   5. _____

Part III
Directions: Answer the questions in complete sentences.

1. Why is DNA sometimes called the "blueprint" of an organism?

_____

_____

_____

2. Explain the relationship between DNA, genes, and chromosomes.

_____

_____

_____

Heredity

The characteristics of all living things are called traits. Every living thing is a collection of **inherited traits** (characteristics passed down to an individual by his or her parents). These traits are controlled by genes made up of DNA and located on the chromosomes. Traits are passed on to new cells during meiosis.

Gregor Mendel was the first person to describe how traits are inherited. His studies of the inherited traits of pea plants led to the **Laws of Dominance** (principles of genetics). He noticed that genes always came in pairs. Every organism that reproduces sexually receives two genes for every trait. A trait may be **dominant** (stronger), and that trait will show up in the organism. If a trait is **recessive** (weaker), it will not show up in the organism unless the organism inherits two recessive genes.

Scientists use a **Punnett square**, designed by Reginald Punnett, to predict all possible gene combinations for the offspring of two parents. The Punnett square consists of four boxes inside a square. Each box represents a possible gene combination. The parents' genes are placed outside the square

Example: This Punnett square shows the cross between two tall pea plants. Each one has one tall gene and one short gene. **T** = Tall gene (dominate trait) and **t** = short gene (recessive trait).

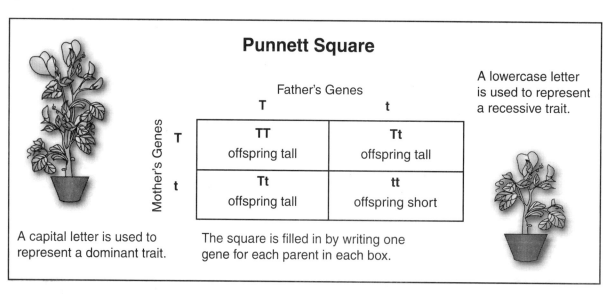

Punnett Square

A lowercase letter is used to represent a recessive trait.

Father's Genes

	T	t
T	**TT** offspring tall	**Tt** offspring tall
t	**Tt** offspring tall	**tt** offspring short

Mother's Genes

A capital letter is used to represent a dominant trait.

The square is filled in by writing one gene for each parent in each box.

Look at the Punnett square for tallness in peas. The genetic makeup of an organism is its genotype. The **genotype** (genetic makeup) of the mother is **Tt**, and the genotype of the father is **Tt**. They each have a tall gene and a short gene, but because the tall gene is dominant, both plants appear tall. There are three possible genotypes for the offspring: **TT**, **Tt**, and **tt**. Using the Punnett square, scientists can predict that 75 percent, or $\frac{3}{4}$, of the offspring will be tall plants. Only a plant that inherits two short genes (**tt**) will be short.

Name: _____ Date: _____

Punnett Square Activity

1. Complete a Punnett square for eye color. The mother has the dominant gene for brown eyes, and her genotype is **BB**. The father has the recessive gene for blue eyes. His genotype is **bb**.

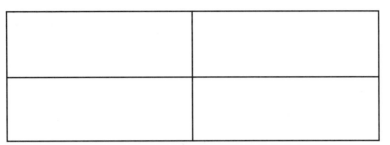

  a.   What are the genotypes possible for eye color for their children? _____

  b.   What percent or fraction of their children will have brown eyes? _____

2. Complete a Punnett square for freckles. The mother has the recessive gene for no freckles. Her genotype is **ff**. The father has the dominant gene for freckles, and his genotype is **Ff**.

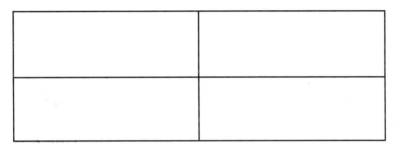

  a.   What are the genotypes possible for freckles for their children? _____

  b.   What percent or fraction of their children will have freckles? _____

3. Complete a Punnett square for dimples. The mother has the recessive gene for no dimples and her genotype is **dd**. The father has the recessive gene for no dimples. His genotype is **dd**.

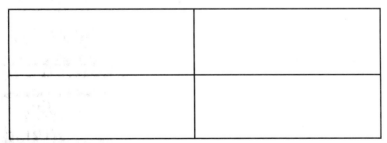

  a.   What are the genotypes possible for dimples for their children? _____

  b.   What percent or fraction of their children will have dimples? _____

Name: _____ Date: _____

Mendelian Traits Activity

Directions: Your **genes** (units in the chromosomes that contain your dominant and recessive traits) have been inherited from your parents and grandparents. Below is a fun list of some common Mendelian traits. Do you have these traits? Which parent also has these traits? Complete the chart.

Mendelian Trait **D** = Dominant trait; **r** = Recessive trait	You	Mother	Father
Tongue Folding (**r**): ability to fold the tip of your tongue back upon the main body of the tongue without using your teeth	*Yes/No*	*Yes/No*	*Yes/No*
Detached Earlobes (**D**): earlobes not directly attached to your head; free-hanging	*Yes/No*	*Yes/No*	*Yes/No*
Attached Earlobes (**r**): earlobes directly attached to the head	*Yes/No*	*Yes/No*	*Yes/No*
Darwin's Tubercle (**D**): bump of cartilage on outer rim of ear	*Yes/No*	*Yes/No*	*Yes/No*
Hitchhiker's Thumb (**D**): thumb, when up in hitchhiking position, can bend backwards at a sharp angle (50% or more)	*Yes/No*	*Yes/No*	*Yes/No*
Dimples (**D**): natural smile produces dimples in one or both cheeks or a dimple in the center of the chin	*Yes/No*	*Yes/No*	*Yes/No*
Widow's Peak (**D**): pull hair off your forehead; hairline comes to a point in the middle of forehead	*Yes/No*	*Yes/No*	*Yes/No*
Bent little finger (**D**): little finger curves in toward other fingers	*Yes/No*	*Yes/No*	*Yes/No*
Webbing (**D**): spread fingers apart; grasp a thumbful of skin	*Yes/No*	*Yes/No*	*Yes/No*
Freckles (**D**): circular pattern of skin coloration	*Yes/No*	*Yes/No*	*Yes/No*
Whorl: The way the hair on the crown of your head turns—clockwise (**D**); counterclockwise (**r**)	*Yes/No*	*Yes/No*	*Yes/No*
Second toe longest (**D**): second toe is longer than the big toe	*Yes/No*	*Yes/No*	*Yes/No*

Apply

What are some of your conclusions about your Mendelian trait inheritance?

_____

_____

_____

_____

Name: _____   Date: _____

Mendelian Traits Activity (cont.)

Complete the chart for your siblings.

Mendelian Trait **D** = Dominant trait; **r** = Recessive trait	**You**	**Mother**	**Father**
Tongue Folding (**r**): ability to fold the tip of your tongue back upon the main body of the tongue without using your teeth	*Yes/No*	*Yes/No*	*Yes/No*
Detached Earlobes (**D**): earlobes not directly attached to your head; free-hanging	*Yes/No*	*Yes/No*	*Yes/No*
Attached Earlobes (**r**): earlobes directly attached to the head	*Yes/No*	*Yes/No*	*Yes/No*
Darwin's Tubercle (**D**): bump of cartilage on outer rim of ear	*Yes/No*	*Yes/No*	*Yes/No*
Hitchhiker's Thumb (**D**): thumb, when up in hitchhiking position, can bend backwards at a sharp angle (50% or more)	*Yes/No*	*Yes/No*	*Yes/No*
Dimples (**D**): natural smile produces dimples in one or both cheeks or a dimple in the center of the chin	*Yes/No*	*Yes/No*	*Yes/No*
Widow's Peak (**D**): pull hair off your forehead; hairline comes to a point in the middle of forehead	*Yes/No*	*Yes/No*	*Yes/No*
Bent little finger (**D**): little finger curves in toward other fingers	*Yes/No*	*Yes/No*	*Yes/No*
Webbing (**D**): spread fingers apart; grasp a thumbful of skin	*Yes/No*	*Yes/No*	*Yes/No*
Freckles (**D**): circular pattern of skin coloration	*Yes/No*	*Yes/No*	*Yes/No*
Whorl: The way the hair on the crown of your head turns—clockwise (**D**); counterclockwise (**r**)	*Yes/No*	*Yes/No*	*Yes/No*
Second toe longest (**D**): second toe is longer than the big toe	*Yes/No*	*Yes/No*	*Yes/No*

Apply

Compare and contrast the results of your survey and the survey of your siblings. Record your observations.

_____

_____

_____

_____

Name: _____ Date: _____

Heredity Review

Part I

Directions: Place the letter of the correct answer on the blanks.

_____ 1. A Punnett square shows possible combinations of:

      a. DNA.   b. chromosomes.   c. genes.   d. cells.

_____ 2. A gene that always show up in the offspring is a:

      a. dominant gene.   b. recessive gene.   c. pure gene.   d. hybrid gene.

_____ 3. Inherited traits are controlled by:

      a. cells.   b. chromosomes.   c. mitosis.   d. genes.

_____ 4. Traits that are passed on from parents to their offspring are called:

      a. inherited traits.   b. recessive genes.   c. genes.   d. genetics.

_____ 5. Genes are located on the:

      a. cell wall.   b. chromosomes.   c. DNA.   d. vacuole.

Part II

Directions: Complete the Punnett square for hair type. Curly hair (**DD**) is dominant to straight hair (**dd**). The mother has curly hair, and her genotype is **DD**. The father has straight hair, and his genotype is **dd**.

1. What are the possible genotypes for hair type for their children? _____

2. What percent or fraction of their children will have curly hair? _____

Part III

Directions: Answer the question in complete sentences.

1. What makes each person a unique individual?

_____

_____

_____

_____

_____

Simple Organisms

Simple organisms—monerans, protests, and fungi—do not have complex structures. This makes them easy for scientists to study using a microscope.

The Kingdom of Monerans

Monerans are one-celled organisms that have no nucleus and no organelles to help them carry on life processes. Some monerans, known as cyanobacteria, are **producers** (can make their own food) and contain chlorophyll. Cyanobacteria can be found in the slimy green stuff found on some ponds and lakes. Fish and other small animals living in or near the water eat these monerans for food. Other monerans are **consumers** (depend on other organisms for their food), and they are known as bacteria. Bacteria live everywhere. They can be helpful by decomposing dead plants and animals, making foods such as vinegar and sauerkraut, and breaking down food in our digestive system.

While some monerans are helpful, **pathogens** (disease-producing monerans) can be very harmful. Lyme disease, strep throat, cholera, and other diseases are pathogens that make many people ill each year. Some monerans produce **toxins** (poisons). Bacteria in spoiled food can produce toxins, causing a disease called botulism. It can affect the nervous system and even kill the person eating the spoiled food.

Cyanobacteria   *Bacteria*

The Kingdom of Fungi

Fungi (the plural of fungus) is responsible for the decay and decomposition of living matter. They are found wherever other living organisms are found. Many kinds of fungus prefer areas that are warm and moist. Fungi need oxygen, water, and food to survive and grow.

Some kinds of fungi are parasites, and they cause harm to their host. They are responsible for many serious plant and animal diseases, such as athlete's foot and ringworm. Other fungi are helpful and have many uses. **Mold** (a kind of fungus) reproduces by **spores** (tiny particles

of matter that are enclosed in walls) and is used to make penicillin and cheese. Yeast is one kind of fungus that reproduces through **budding** (a new organism develops on the parent, it matures, and breaks away) and is used to make bread. The yeast changes the sugars in the dough into **carbon dioxide** (a gas), causing the dough to rise.

Basidiomycete
(mushroom)

Zygomycete
(black bread mold)

Simple Organisms (cont.)

The Kingdom of Protists

Protist cells have a nucleus and organelles that help the nucleus perform all the life processes. Protista can be unicellular or multicellular. Protista can be producers, consumers, or **decomposers** (break down matter and use the nutrients). Protista like moist and wet environments. They move about in their watery homes by using **cilia** (hair-like structures), **pseudopodia** (false feet), or **flagella** (whip-like structures).

Three Groups of Protists

Groups	Characteristics	Examples	Harmful or Helpful?
Protozoa *Animal-like*	- some are consumers - most are unicellular - many are **parasites** (live off another organism, causing that host some harm)	- amoeba - paramecium	**Causes:** - dysentery - sleeping sickness - malaria
Algae *Plant-like*	- producers - contain chlorophyll and can make their own food	- euglena - diatom - kelp - red and green algae	**Used in making:** - toothpaste - dairy products - ice cream - fertilizer - oxygen
Fungus-like	- decomposers	- slime mold - mildew - white rust	- cause food spoilage - used in making cheese and penicillin

Name: _____ Date: _____

Simple Organism Activities

Disease Research

Directions: Research a disease listed below. Using your research, create a public service announcement about the disease that includes the organism responsible for the disease, the manner in which it is transmitted, and the major symptoms.

whooping cough	tuberculosis	tetanus	diphtheria
scarlet fever	strep throat	pneumonia	cholera
anthrax	botulism	Lyme disease	

Bacteria Research

Directions: Harmful bacteria are all around us. There are many ways to control the growth of these harmful monerans. Research one of the topics listed below. Using the information, create a poster promoting the use of this method to fight disease and sickness caused by bacteria.

antibiotics	antibodies	antiseptic	vaccines
refrigeration	dehydration	sterilization	vacuum packing
freezing	disinfectant		

Mushroom Research

Directions: Some people hunt wild mushrooms in the spring and then fry them up as a special treat for dinner. Some kinds of mushrooms are poisonous. It is important to know the difference between a good mushroom and a poisonous one. Research each kind of mushroom below. Use the information to create a pamphlet for mushroom hunters that will help them identify edible and poisonous mushrooms.

chanterelle	king boletus	morel	oyster mushroom
amanitas	death angel	truffle	sulfur mushroom
death cap	shaggy mane	giant puffball	Jack-o-lantern

Taste-Testing Party
(Check with parents/guardians about food allergies.)

Directions: Many of the foods we eat are made using bacteria and fungi. Gather a variety of foods that are made with bacteria. After tasting each kind of food, rate each food, with "1" being good and "5" worst.

buttermilk	1 2 3 4 5	cheddar cheese	1 2 3 4 5
yogurt	1 2 3 4 5	Swiss cheese	1 2 3 4 5
sour cream	1 2 3 4 5	American cheese	1 2 3 4 5
sourdough bread	1 2 3 4 5	yogurt smoothie	1 2 3 4 5
yeast rolls	1 2 3 4 5	Mozzarella cheese	1 2 3 4 5

Name: _____ Date: _____

Protist Lab

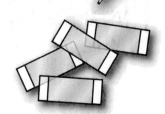

Purpose: Identify organisms found in a variety of water sources

Materials Needed

microscope   eyedropper
cover slips   slides
variety of water samples: pond, river, tap, bottled, and others

Procedure

Step 1: Label water samples.
Step 2: Place one drop of water from each sample on separate slides.
Step 3: Place a cover slip over each drop of water.

Observation

View water under the microscope. Draw any microorganisms present in the water.

Pond Water	River Water
Bottled Water	Tap Water
Other Sample	Other Sample

Research

Directions: Identify each organism you found in the water samples. Label your drawings with the correct organism name.

Name: _____   Date: _____

Yeast Reproduction Lab

Purpose: Observe reproduction of yeast cells

Materials Needed

yeast	glass beaker or jar	sugar	warm water
eyedropper	microscope	slides	cover slips
magnifying glass			

Part I

Procedure

Step 1: Place yeast on a slide and view with a magnifying glass.

Observation

_____

_____

_____

_____

Part II

Procedure

Step 1: Place yeast and sugar in a beaker.
Step 2: Pour warm water into the beaker.
Step 3: Let the mixture sit for 10 minutes.

Observation

1. What did you observe happening in the beaker? Record your observations.

_____

_____

_____

_____

2. Place a drop of yeast mixture onto a slide and view under the microscope. Record your observations.

_____

_____

_____

_____

Name: _____ Date: _____

Mold Garden Lab

Purpose: Identify conditions molds need to survive and grow

Materials Needed

1 can of tomato soup	3 clear plastic cups
bread crumbs	soil
magnifying glass	plastic wrap

Procedure

Step 1: Number each cup and pour $\frac{1}{2}$ cup of soup into each.

Step 2: Sprinkle bread crumbs into cup #1.

Step 3: Sprinkle soil into cup #2.

Step 4: Run your finger across a dusty or dirty surface in the classroom. Dip your finger into cup #3.

Step 5: Seal each cup with plastic wrap and place in a dark, warm cabinet or closet for three days.

Observation

After three days, view the cups using a magnifying glass and record your observations.

_____

_____

_____

_____

Conclusion

What does mold need to live and grow?

_____

_____

_____

_____

Name: _____ Date: _____

Simple Organisms Review

Part I
Directions: Match the definitions with the correct vocabulary words.

_____ 1. producers

_____ 2. consumers

_____ 3. decomposers

_____ 4. mold

_____ 5. protozoa

a. break down matter and use the nutrients

b. depend on other organisms for their food

c. amoeba

d. organisms that can make their own food

e. penicillin

Part II
Directions: Write the letter of the correct answer on the line.

_____ 1. Monerans that produce disease are known as _____.
   a. pathogens   b. toxins   c. botulism   d. antibodies

_____ 2. Some protists use pseudopodia, or _____.
   a. cilia   b. flagella   c. false feet   d. algae

_____ 3. Malaria is caused by a(n) _____.
   a. algae   b. mold   c. white rust   d. protozoa

_____ 4. Some bacteria produce toxins or _____.
   a. antibodies   b. poisons   c. dysentery   d. cyanobacteria

_____ 5. Most protists live in _____ environments.
   a. dry   b. moist   c. soil   d. rocky

Part III
Directions: Answer the questions in complete sentences.

1. Explain how some monerans can be classified as producers.

   _____

   _____

   _____

   _____

2. Why are monerans, protists, and fungi called simple organisms?

   _____

   _____

   _____

   _____

Plant Kingdom

Plants are multicellular organisms. Plants make their own food in a process called photosynthesis. Because plants can make their own food, scientists classify them as producers. Plants can be divided into two major groups: **vascular** (having tube-like structures inside the plant to carry food, water, and minerals) and **nonvascular** (no tube-like structures to carry food and water through the plant).

Vascular plants do not need as much direct contact with water. As a result, they are able to grow in almost every kind of environment. Vascular plants produce leaves, stems, and roots. The leaves make food for the plant with the help of sunlight and chlorophyll. The **xylem** (water-transporting tissues) and **phloem** (tissue responsible for moving food down from the leaves to other parts of the plant) carry water to the leaves and food to all parts of the plant. They include plants such as maple trees, tomatoes, and roses.

Nonvascular plants do not have leaves, stems, or roots. Most nonvascular plants are found in moist areas. They include mosses, hornworts, and liverworts.

Plant Kingdom	Examples
Vascular Plants - grow almost everywhere - leaves, stems, roots - have xylem and phloem tissue	
Nonvascular Plants - most found in moist areas - do not have stems or roots - do not have xylem and phloem tissue	

Name: _____ Date: _____

Vascular Plant Lab

Purpose: Explore the role of stems in the transporting of water in vascular plants

Materials Needed

one stalk of celery with leaves   glass beaker or jar   water
magnifying glass   red food coloring

Part I
Procedure

Step 1: Fill the glass beaker half full of water.
Step 2: Add several drops of red food coloring to the water.
Step 3: Cut one inch off the end of the celery stalk and discard.
Step 4: Place the celery stalk in the beaker of water.

Observation

After 24 hours, view the celery stalk and record your observations.

_____

_____

_____

Part II
Procedure

Step 1: Cut off another inch piece from the bottom of the celery stalk.
Step 2: Use a magnifying glass to examine the piece of celery.

Observation

Draw your observations.

Part III
Procedure

Cut the remaining celery stalk lengthwise and observe the structures.

Apply

Is celery a vascular or nonvascular plant? Explain your answer.

_____

_____

_____

Parts of Plants

Vascular plants have three main parts: roots, leaves, and stems.

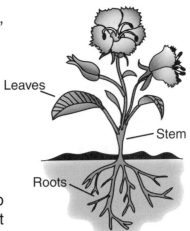

Leaves

Stem

Roots

Roots

Roots anchor the plant in the ground. They absorb water and minerals from the soil with the help of tiny root hairs. The root also stores extra food for the plant.

Types of Root	Example
fibrous root: many roots are attached to the plant and they spread out	grass tree
taproot: large root growing straight down in the ground	carrot radish

Stems

Stems support the plant and hold the leaves up to the light. They also transport water from the roots and food from the leaves to other parts of the plant. Stems contain three basic types of tissue: **xylem** (tissue responsible for moving water up from the roots to the other parts of the plant), **phloem** (tissue responsible for moving food down from the leaves to the other parts of the plant), and **cambium** (growth tissue that makes new xylem and phloem).

Types of Stems	Example
herbaceous: soft and bendable stems	roses corn plants
woody: hard stems that do not bend easily	maple trees

Name: _____ Date: _____

Root Growth Lab

Purpose: Identify the function of root hairs

Materials Needed

large sweet potato   glass or jar

water   toothpicks

Procedure

Step 1: Place a sweet potato in the jar or glass of water.

Step 2: Keep the top half of the potato out of the water by placing toothpicks into the sides of the potato. The toothpicks will rest on the side of the jar.

Step 3: Place the sweet potato in a sunny location.

Step 4: Add water to the jar as needed.

Observation

Record your observation of the plant's growth over a period of several months.

_____

_____

_____

_____

Conclusion

Examine the root hairs of the sweet potato plant. Why do you think a plant might need so many root hairs?

_____

_____

_____

_____

Name: _____ Date: _____

Plant Stem Lab

Purpose: Identify the function of the plant stem

Materials Needed

white, long-stemmed carnation   water

red and blue food coloring   2 glass beakers or jars

knife

Procedure

Step 1: Fill the 2 beakers or jars ¾ full of water.

Step 2: Add several drops of red food coloring to one beaker or jar and blue food coloring to the second beaker or jar.

Step 3: Slice the stem of the flower lengthwise, stopping 3 inches below the flower.

Step 4: Place one end of the stem in the beaker of red water and the other in the beaker of blue water.

Step 5: Place the flower in a sunny place.

Observation

After 24 hours, observe the flower and record your observations.

_____

_____

_____

_____

Conclusion

How does water get from the roots to the flower and leaves of a plant?

_____

_____

_____

_____

Leaves

Leaves have one very important job to do; they make the food that the plant needs to stay alive. Most leaves have two important parts: the blade and the petiole. The blade of the leaf has several important parts: cuticle, veins, guard cells, and stomata.

Parts of a Leaf

blade: flat, thin green part of the leaf

cuticle: layer that keeps too much water from evaporating from the leaf

petiole: stalk or stem that attaches the blade to the stem of the plant

stomata: tiny openings in the leaf

veins: tubes that transport food and water throughout the leaf; they also support the leaf

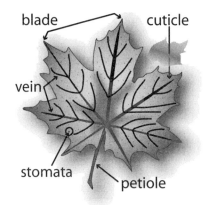

Layers of Leaves

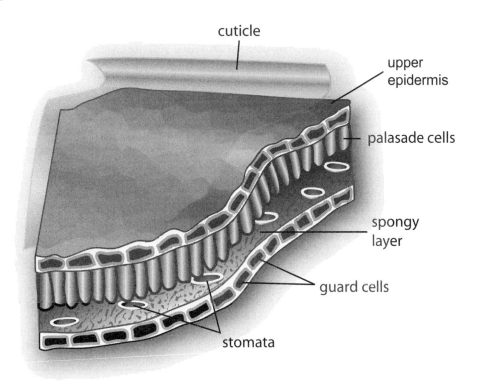

Shapes of Leaves

Leaves have the same basic parts, but they are not all put together in the same way.

Kinds of Leaves	Examples
simple leaf: one blade attached to a single petiole	
compound leaves: more than one blade attached to a single petiole	Pinnated leaves Palmated Leaves

Leaf Veins

Leaves are really bundles of xylem and phloem tubes needed to transport food and water throughout the leaf. These tubes or veins have another important job to do. They support the leaf and hold it up so that as much surface as possible can be exposed to the sun. That helps the plant make as much food as possible.

Veins in Leaves	Examples
parallel veins: veins are side by side to each other, running from the base of the leaf to the tip of the leaf	
net-veined leaves: single main vein with smaller veins branching off of it	

Leaf Attachments

Alternating Leaves	
Spiraling Leaves	
Oppositional Leaves	
Decussate Leaves	
Whorled Leaves	

Leaf Collection Activity

Directions: Create a leaf book. Collect examples of simple and compound leaves, parallel and net-veined leaves, and different types of leaf attachments. Place each leaf sample between sheets of newspaper. Place the leaves in between the pages of a telephone book or other heavy book. After several days, take the leaves out of the telephone book and separate them from the newspaper. The leaves will be flat and dry. Place each leaf sample between two sheets of wax paper. Then place the leaf and wax paper between the two sheets of newspapers. Press the paper with a very warm iron. This will seal the leaf between the wax paper. Glue the sealed leaves to white construction paper and label. Design a cover for the leaf book, add the leaf pages, and staple.

Food Factory of Plants

Photosynthesis (the process plants use to make food) happens in the leaf. The green leaves absorb light energy from the sun. They also take in carbon dioxide from the air through the **stomata** (tiny openings in the leaves). Water and minerals from the soil travel through the roots and stems of the plant to combine with **chlorophyll** (the green chemical in the leaf that allows plants to trap the sun's energy), sunlight, and carbon dioxide to produce **glucose** (sugar). Glucose is the usable food for green plants.

Photosynthesis

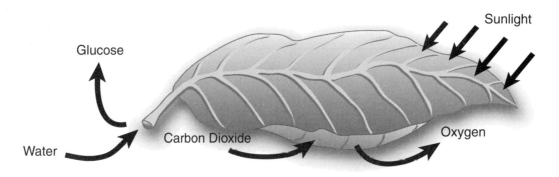

Respiration and Transpiration

Respiration, the exchange of gases and water between plants and the atmosphere, is a continuous cycle. Respiration is important to the process of making glucose. The plant takes in carbon dioxide and gives off oxygen through the stomata during photosynthesis. During **transpiration** (evaporation of water from a plant) the water the plant does not need for photosynthesis is released into the atmosphere through the stomata.

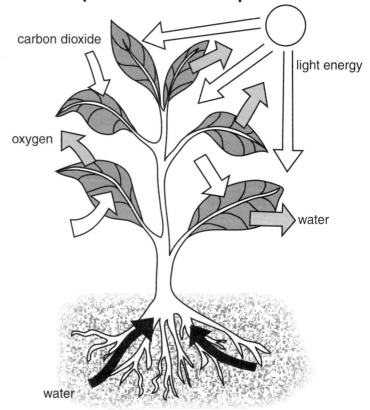

Name: _____ Date: _____

Sunlight and Photosynthesis Lab

Purpose: Understand that plants need sunlight to make food

Materials Needed

geranium plant   aluminum foil

Procedure

Step 1: Cover one leaf with aluminum foil.

Step 2: Set the plant in a sunny place.

Step 3: Water the plant when needed.

Observation

After a week, remove the aluminum foil from the leaf. Record your observations.

_____

_____

_____

_____

Conclusion

1. Why was covering the leaf with foil harmful to the plant?

    _____

    _____

    _____

    _____

2. Explain what you would expect to happen if a plant was left in a dark room.

    _____

    _____

    _____

    _____

Name: _____   Date: _____

Chlorophyll Lab

Purpose: Identify the green substance in plant leaves

Materials Needed

1 cup green tree leaves torn into pieces   small glass beaker or jar

deep baking dish half full of very hot (not boiling) water   rubbing alcohol

Procedure

Step 1: Place leaves into glass beaker or jar.

Step 2: Add enough rubbing alcohol to jar to cover the leaves.

Step 3: Place beaker in hot water and let sit for thirty minutes. Replace hot water if needed.

Observation

Remove the beaker from the water. Record your observations.

_____

_____

_____

_____

Conclusion

Why did the alcohol turn green?

_____

_____

_____

_____

Apply

Why do leaves turn colors in the fall?

_____

_____

_____

_____

Name: _____ Date: _____

Plant Respiration Lab

Purpose: Understand that plants exchange gases with the atmosphere

Materials Needed

geranium plant   tree leaves

petroleum jelly   magnifying glass

Part I

Procedure

Look at the underside of a tree leaf with a magnifying glass. If you look closely, you will see small pin-size holes.

Part II

Procedure

Step 1: Cover the bottom of a leaf of the geranium plant with a thin layer of petroleum jelly.

Step 2: Set the plant in a sunny place for a few days.

Step 3: Water the plant when needed.

Observation

After a week, record your observations.

_____

_____

_____

_____

Conclusion

What caused the leaf to wilt and die?

_____

_____

_____

_____

Name: _____ Date: _____

Transpiration in Plants Lab

Purpose: Understand that plants release water into the atmosphere through small openings in the leaf

Materials

magnifying glass   large tree leaves
green plant with large leaves   plastic bag

Part I

Procedure

Look at the underside of a tree leaf with a magnifying glass. If you look closely, you will see small pin-size holes.

Part II

Procedure

Step 1: Place a plastic bag over a leaf of a green plant. Loosely tie the bag to the leaf stem.

Step 2: Leave the bag on the plant for several days.

Observation

After a week, record your observations.

_____

_____

_____

_____

Conclusion

Explain how this activity demonstrates the process of plant transpiration.

_____

_____

_____

_____

How Plants Reproduce

Plants reproduce in two ways.

Method of Reproduction	Examples
sexual: joining two cells, male cell and female cell, making a new organism in a process called fertilization	- flowers - cones - spores
asexual: reproduction that does not involve male and female cells combining	- budding - eyes - runners - bulbs

Scientists divide plants that reproduce sexually into two groups.

Classification	Type of Seed	Examples
Angiosperms: flowering plants	- seeds are surrounded by the tissues that eventually become fruits	- maple trees - daises
Gymnosperms: nonflowering plants	- produce seeds inside cones - spores	- fir trees, spruce - ferns, mosses

Flowering Plants

Flowers perform the job of reproduction for the plant. The **pistil** (female reproductive part of the flower) consists of the stigma, style, ovary, and egg cells. The **stamen** (male reproductive part of a flower) contains the anther, filament, and **pollen** (sperm cells).

Pollination

Pollination (the movement of pollen from one plant to another) is necessary for seeds to form in flowering plants. The stamen is the male reproductive part of a flower. The stamen consists of two parts: the filament and the anther. Some flowers are **self-pollinators** (have everything they need to pollinate in just one plant). The pollen grains will travel from the stamens of the plant to the pistil of the same plant. Other flowers are **cross-pollinators** (need another plant to make the pollination complete). Cross-pollinators often have large colorful blooms. They may have a sweet scent and sweeter nectar. They attract insects and birds to their flowers. These animals pick up the pollen grains while feeding and carry them to another flower.

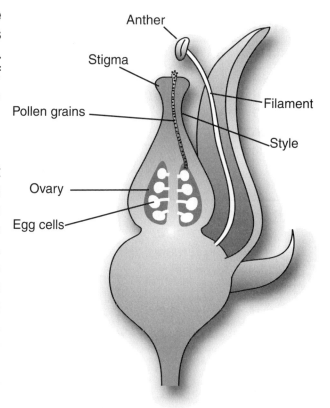

Flowers become fruit after pollination. Fruit provides a covering for seeds. Fruit can be fleshy like an apple or hard like a nut.

Name: _____   Date: _____

Dissecting a Flower Lab

Procedure: Identify the parts of a flower

Materials Needed

large flowers   toothpick

magnifying glass   black paper

clear tape

Procedure

Step 1: Open up the flower gently with your hands.

Step 2: Locate each of the flower parts listed below.

Step 3: Carefully separate each part from the flower and tape it in the correct box.

petal	anther	filament
sepal	eggs	pistil

Observation

Brush the anther against the black paper. Using the magnifying glass, look at the black paper. Record your observations.

_____

_____

_____

Seeds

In flowering plants, seeds form in the fruit. Seeds have three parts: **seed coat** (protects new plant inside seed), **embryo** (new plant), and the **cotyledon** (seed leaves). Most seeds are **monocots** (having one cotyledon) or **dicots** (having two cotyledons).

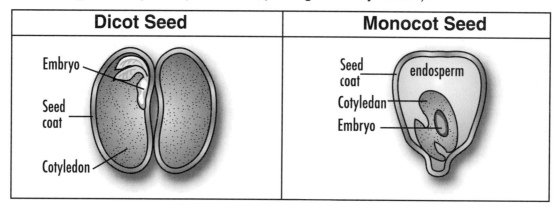

Dicot Seed	Monocot Seed
Embryo, Seed coat, Cotyledon	Seed coat, endosperm, Cotyledan, Embryo

Characteristics of Dicot and Monocot Plant

Characteristic	Dicot	Monocot
flower	- four or five petals or multiples of four or five	- three petals or multiples of three
leaves	- branching veins	- parallel veins
roots	- taproot	- fibrous

Seed Germination

　　Germination (early growth of a plant from a seed) depends on three factors: temperature, moisture, and oxygen. When the three conditions are right, the seed opens, and the embryo emerges.

Name: _____   Date: _____

Seed Germination Lab

Purpose: Identify requirements for seed germination

Materials Needed

24 bean seeds   six glass jars
paper towels   water

Procedure

Step 1: Number each jar. Place a paper towel around the inside of each jar.
Step 2: Place four seeds between the paper towel and the side of each jar.
Step 3: Moisten the paper towel in jars 1, 2, and 3. Leave the paper towel dry in jars 4, 5, and 6.
Step 4: Place the jars in a warm, sunny location. Keep paper towels in jars 1–3 moist.

Observation

Observe and record the changes in the seeds for 2 weeks.
Week 1

_____

_____

_____

Week 2

_____

_____

_____

Conclusion

1. What is the job of water in seed germination?

_____

_____

_____

2. What do seeds need for germination?

_____

_____

_____

Name: _____   Date: _____

Monocot and Dicot Seed Lab

Purpose: Compare and contrast monocot and dicot seeds

Materials Needed

lima beans

corn seeds

toothpicks

magnifying glass

Procedure

Step 1: Soak seeds in water for 24 hours before beginning lab.

Step 2: Teacher prepares corn seeds for students by slicing them in half.

Step 3: Peel the seed coat off the bean seed. Gently pry the seed apart using your thumbnail or the toothpick.

Observation

Observe the corn and the bean seeds using the magnifying glass. Draw a picture of each seed and label the parts.

Bean Seed	Corn Seed

Conclusion

Compare and contrast monocot and dicot seeds.

_____

_____

_____

_____

Name: _____ Date: _____

Monocot and Dicot Plant Activity

Directions: Identify the flowering plants below as dicot or monocot using the information in the chart on page 46. Examine each picture: count the petals, look at the vein patterns, or determine the root system. Write the answer on the line under each picture.

1. _____ 2. _____ 3. _____

4. _____ 5. _____ 6. _____

7. _____ 8. _____ 9. _____

Trees

Trees are plants with woody stems. The stem or trunk of the tree contains three basic types of tissue: xylem, phloem, and cambium. The xylem and phloem tissues in trees form rings around the stems. Each year another layer of xylem and phloem is made for the plant. The older layers form growth rings, one for every year that the plant has been alive. By counting the growth rings on a tree, an observer can determine not only how old the tree is, but what the weather was like during its lifetime. In years with plenty of rain, the growth ring will be thick. In years with lighter rains, the growth ring will be narrow.

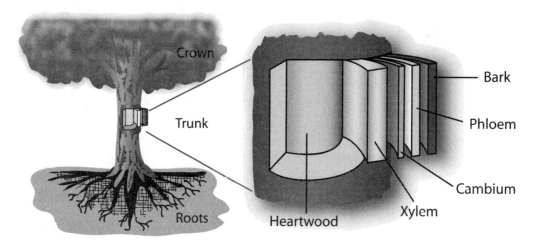

Two Types of Trees

Gymnosperms are plants that have true leaves, stems, and roots. They have a vascular system, or tubes, to carry food and water to all parts of the plant. They reproduce by making seeds. Many gymnosperm plants are called conifers because they produce their seeds inside cones. **Coniferous** (needle leaf) trees have green needles the year-round. These trees are also called evergreens. Redwood trees, the tallest and one of the oldest trees known in the world, are gymnosperms. Gymnosperms grow in a number of places. They can be found in huge evergreen forests, and they can be found as decorative plants in the lawns of homes and businesses. They are important to the lumber and paper industry because they are fast-growing plants.

Angiosperms are plants with true leaves, stems, and roots; they also have a vascular system. This is a very large group that contains more than half of all the plants in the world. They reproduce by making seeds inside of fruits. People eat the fruits of many of the angiosperms, such as apples and peaches. We do not even notice some of the flowers and fruit. Most **deciduous** (broadleaf) trees, such as maples, oaks, and elms, flower in the spring. The flowers may be the same color as the leaves, so we do not always notice them. The green leaves of the deciduous trees stop making food in the fall and are shed by the trees.

Name: _____ Date: _____

Tree Activities

Tree Identification Pamphlet Activity

Directions: Create a tree identification pamphlet for beginner home gardeners. The information should help readers understand the difference between angiosperm and gymnosperm plants, define coniferous and deciduous, and include pictures or drawings of both types of trees.

Tree Folder Activity

Directions: Make a folder book. Fold a sheet of construction paper vertically in half, like a hot dog bun. Unfold the paper. Fold the bottom edge of the paper up to form a two-inch pocket and staple each side. Label one side of the folder "Coniferous Trees" and the other side "Deciduous Trees." Using magazines and seed catalogs, cut out pictures of trees and place them in the correct pocket of the folder.

Tree Cube Activity

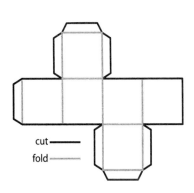

cut ——
fold ------

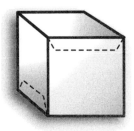

Directions: Choose a tree to research. Use the information to complete a tree cube. Identify the tree as angiosperm or gymnosperm and coniferous or deciduous. Include pictures or drawings of the tree, its leaves, fruit, nuts, seeds, and other important details about the plant. Cut out the cube shape, fold, and tape the sides together.

Tree Rings Activity

Directions: Count the rings of a **tree cookie** (cross section) to determine the history of the tree.

Rules:
1. Each ring represents one year of growth.
2. The bark and center ring are not counted.
3. The youngest ring is closest to the bark.
4. Rings close together indicate poor conditions for growth:
   - not enough water
   - overcrowding
   - disease
   - insect attack
5. Irregular or oval shape of rings indicates the tree leaned over or was blocked while growing in some way.
6. Rings far apart indicate good conditions for growth:
   - plenty of water
   - minerals
   - light

Name: _____   Date: _____

Plant Review

Part I
Directions: Match the definitions with the correct vocabulary words.

_____ 1. photosynthesis

_____ 2. stomata

_____ 3. deciduous trees

_____ 4. gymnosperms

_____ 5. taproot

a. broadleaf trees

b. large root growing straight down

c. non-flowering plants

d. process plants use to make food

e. opening in the leaf

Part II
Directions: Write the letter of the correct answer on the line.

_____ 1. The part of the stem that carries water and nutrients to the leaves is the:
     a. phloem.   b. leaves.   c. roots.   d. xylem.

_____ 2. Evaporation of water from the leaf is called:
     a. respiration. b. transpiration. c. photosynthesis. d. pollination.

_____ 3. The female reproductive part of the flower is called the:
     a. petal.   b. anther.   c. pistil.   d. stamen.

_____ 4. In flowering plants, seeds form in the:
     a. embryo.   b. seed coat.   c. fruit.   d. leaves.

_____ 5. Plants store food in the:
     a. leaf.   b. stem.   c. flower.   d. root.

Part III
Explain how green plants make their food.

_____

_____

_____

_____

Part IV
Directions: Use a Venn diagram to compare and contrast angiosperms and gymnosperms.

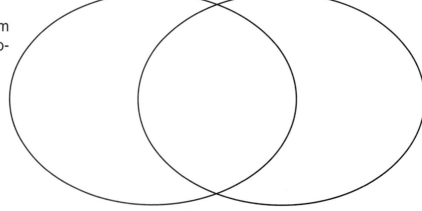

Name: _____ Date: _____

Animal Kingdom

The animal kingdom, while diverse, can be divided into two main categories. These categories encompass all animals. They are **invertebrates** (animals without backbones) and **vertebrates** (animals with backbones). Within the categories of vertebrate and invertebrate, there are several subcategories that further classify the animals.

Invertebrates

Invertebrates make up a large part of the animal kingdom. They can live on land, or they can live in the water. Invertebrates are subdivided by their structure and form.

Invertebrate Graphic Organizer

Directions: Using the chart on the next page, complete the graphic organizer with examples for each type of invertebrate.

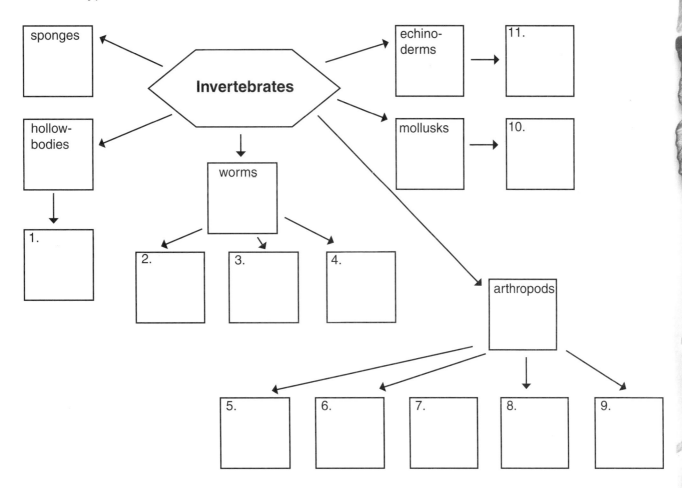

Invertebrates (cont.)

Types	Characteristics	Examples
Sponges	- simplest invertebrate - body two layers of cells thick - simple supporting structure - hollow tube-shaped body with opening at the top	- sponges
Hollow-bodies	- opening at top of tube-shaped body surrounded by tentacles - tentacles grasp food and bring to mouth - tentacles used for defense	- microscopic hydra, jellyfish, sea anemones, and corals *jellyfish*
Worms	- simple digestive systems - simple brain - smell receptors - ear spots - sense of touch - sense of taste - includes flatworms, roundworms, and segmented worms	- flatworms, roundworms, and segmented worms *segmented worms* *roundworms* *flatworm*
Mollusks	- live in water or wet areas - some have soft bodies - some have protective shells - lack segments and legs	- snails, slugs, scallops, oysters, clams, nautilus, and octopus *oyster*
Arthropods	- divided bodies; each segment has a specific function - jointed legs - **exoskeleton** (hard outer shell that protects the body)	- arachnids, crustaceans, centipedes, millipedes, and insects *water strider* *beetle*
Echinoderms	- spiny-skinned - marine animals - central body - arms in multiples of five - supporting skeletal structure just under skin	- starfish, brittle star, sea urchins, sand dollars, and sea cucumbers *sand dollar* *starfish*

Vertebrates

Vertebrates (animals with backbones) are divided into five groups. Each group has its own unique characteristics.

Types	Characteristics	Examples
Fish	- gills - lay eggs - **cold-blooded** (body temperature that changes with the temperature of its surroundings)	Angelfish Shark
Amphibians	- most young have gills - most adults have lungs - lay eggs in water or moist ground - cold-blooded	Leopard Frog Fire Newt
Reptiles	- dry scaly skin - eggs have tough skin - cold blooded	Rattlesnake Iguana
Birds	- have feathers - have wings - lay eggs - **warm-blooded** (constant body temperature)	Flamingo Mourning Dove
Mammals	- hair at some point in life - young drink mother's milk - warm-blooded	Elk Ferret

Vertebrate Sorting Activity

Directions: Cut apart the cards below. Using the five groups as guides, sort all the animal pictures into the correct category.

Fish	Amphibians	Birds	Reptiles
Mammals			

Name: _____ Date: _____

Animal Kingdom Review

Part I

Directions: Use the words from the word bank to fill in the blanks.

tentacles	exoskeleton	hollow-bodies	sponge
worms	mollusks	arthropods	echinoderms
cold-blooded	fish	amphibians	reptile
birds	mammals	warm-blooded	invertebrates

1. Some _____ have protective shells.

2. _____ help hollow-bodied invertebrates bring food to their mouths.

3. All _____ have hair at some point in their lives.

4. _____ have simple digestive systems.

5. _____ have feathers and lay eggs.

6. Reptiles, fish, and amphibians are _____.

7. An animal that keeps a constant body temperature is _____.

8. _____ lay eggs in water or on moist ground.

9. A _____'s body is only two layers of cells thick.

10. An _____ is a hard outer shell that protects the body.

11. _____ have sub-categories that include arachnids, crustaceans, centipedes, millipedes, and insects.

12. _____ have arms in multiples of 5.

13. _____ use tentacles for defense.

14. _____ have gills.

15. A _____ egg has tough outer skin.

16. _____ have no internal skeletal system.

Part II

Directions: Fill in the blank with T if the statement is true or an F if the statement is false.

_____ 1. Flatworms, round worms, and segmented worms are all invertebrates.

_____ 2. All mammals are cold-blooded.

_____ 3. Reptiles drink their mother's milk.

_____ 4. A starfish is an echinoderm.

_____ 5. Most adult amphibians have lungs.

Part III

Directions: Answer the question in complete sentences.
What is the purpose of the exoskeleton?

_____

_____

_____

_____

Scientist Bookmark

Directions: Research one of the people from the list. Using this information, fill in the blanks on the bookmark. On the other side of the bookmark create an illustration that represents the important contribution the person made to science. Cut out the bookmark. Punch a hole at the top, run yarn through the hole, and tie.

- ◆ Hans Janssen
- ◆ Zacharias Janssen
- ◆ Robert Hooke
- ◆ Anton van Leeuwenhoek
- ◆ Matthias Schleiden
- ◆ Randolph Virchow
- ◆ Theodor Schwann
- ◆ Gregor Mendel
- ◆ Frederick Griffith
- ◆ Oswald Avery
- ◆ Rosalind Franklin
- ◆ James Watson
- ◆ Francis Crick
- ◆ Reginald Punnett
- ◆ Emil Adolph von Behring
- ◆ Ferdinand Julius Cohn
- ◆ René Jules Dubos
- ◆ Sir Alexander Fleming
- ◆ Kitasato Shibasaburo
- ◆ Robert Koch
- ◆ Louis Pasteur
- ◆ Rachel Carson
- ◆ Luther Burbank
- ◆ George Washington Carver
- ◆ Albert Claude
- ◆ Jacques Cousteau
- ◆ Benjamin Duggar
- ◆ Dian Fossey
- ◆ Jane Goodall
- ◆ Albert Sabin
- ◆ Howard Temin
- ◆ Gerty Cori

(name of scientist)

Birth date: _____

Death date: _____

Nationality: _____

Important Facts

1. _____
_____
_____
_____

2. _____
_____
_____
_____

Important Scientific Contributions

_____
_____
_____
_____
_____
_____
_____

Name:_____

Unit One: Glossary

adapted: suited

algae: plant-like organism

anatomy: structure

angiosperms: flowering plants

asexual: reproduction that does not involve male and female cells combining

blade: flat, thin, green part of the leaf

botanist: a person who studies plants

budding: new organism develops on parent, matures, and breaks away

cambium: growth tissue that makes new xylem and phloem

carbon dioxide: a gas used by plants in photosynthesis

cell membrane: a thin layer that encloses the cell and controls what enters and leaves the cell

cell wall: surrounds cell membrane in plants; provides shape and support

cells: smallest living things

centromere: middle of a chromosome

chloroplast: disc-shaped organelle in plant cells; gives plants their green color; contains chlorophyll that helps plants make food

chlorophyll: green chemical in the leaf that allows plants to trap the sun's energy

chromosomes: rod-shaped strands containing genetic material

cilia: hair-like structures

classify: organize

cold-blooded: organism whose body temperature changes with the temperature of its surroundings

compound leaves: more than one blade attached to a single petiole

coniferous: needle leaf; conebearing plants

consumers: use other organisms as their food

cross-pollinators: need another plant to complete pollination

cotyledon: seed leaves

cuticle: layer that keeps too much water from evaporating from the leaf

cytoplasm: a gel-like material that contains proteins, nutrients, and all of the other cell organelles

daughter cells: two new cells formed during mitosis and meiosis

deciduous: broadleaf; loses leaves in the fall

decomposers: break down matter and absorb the nutrients into their cells

dicots: having two cotyledons

diffusion: the movement of molecules into and out of the cell

DNA: molecule in chromosome that contains genetic information

dominant: stronger

embryo: new plant

endoplasmic reticulum: network of tubes that makes up the transportation system for the cell

environment: surroundings

exoskeleton: hard outer shell that protects the body

fertilization: the sperm cell joins the egg

fibrous root: many roots attached to a plant, spread out

flagella: whip-like structure

function: job

gametes: reproductive cells formed during meiosis with half the number of chromosomes as regular cells; egg and sperm

genes: units in the chromosomes that contain the dominant and recessive traits

genetic blueprint: code

genomes: daughter cells; the result of cell reproduction in mitosis

genotype: genetic makeup

glucose: sugar

Golgi bodies: package and distribute protein outside the cell

guard cells: open and close the stomata

gymnosperms: non-flowering plants

herbaceous: soft and bendable stems

heredity: passing physical and character traits from one generation to another

host: an animal or plant that nourishes and supports a parasite or another organism

inherited traits: characteristics passed by the parents

invertebrates: animals without backbones

kingdoms: groups

Laws of Dominance: principles of genetics

meiosis: process of sex cell formation

microbes: microscopic organisms

microscopic organisms: organisms too small to be seen with the unaided eye

mitochondria: organelles that make energy for the cell

mitosis: the process of cell division for growth and repair

mold: a kind of fungus that reproduces by spores

molecules: very small substances; smallest particle of a substance that retains the properties of that substance

monerans: single-celled organisms that do not have a nucleus

monocots: having one cotyledon

multicellular: made up of many cells

net-veined leaves: single main vein with smaller veins branching off

nonvascular: not having tube-like structures to carry food and water through the plant

nucleus: control center for the cell

organelles: many tiny structures in the cytoplasm; each does a specific job for the cell

organisms: living things

osmosis: movement of water molecules into and out of a cell

parallel veins: veins are side by side to each other, running from the base of the leaf to the tip of the leaf

parasites: live off another organism, causing that host some harm

pathogens: disease-producing monerans

petiole: stalk or stem that attaches the blade of a leaf to the stem of the plant

phloem: tissue responsible for moving food down from the leaves to other parts of the plant

photosynthesis: process plants use to make food

pistil: female reproductive part of the flower

pollen: sperm cells

pollination: the pollen from the stamen travels to the pistil

producers: able to capture the sun's energy to make their own food

properties: characteristics that describe an object

protozoa: animal-like organism

pseudopodia: false feet

Punnett square: chart for diagraming how Mendelian traits are passed from parents to offspring

recessive: weaker

respiration: exchange of gases between the plant and the atmosphere

ribosomes: organelles that make protein for the cell

seed coat: protects new plant inside the seed

self-pollinators: have everything they need to pollinate in just one plant

sexual: joining a male cell and a female cell to make a new organism in a process called fertilization

simple leaf: one blade attached to a single petiole

simple organisms: monerans, protists, and fungi

spores: tiny particles of matter that are enclosed in walls

stamen: male reproductive part of a flower

stomata: tiny openings in the leaf of a plant

taproot: large root growing straight down in the ground

theory: an idea that is repeatedly supported by test results

toxins: poisons

traits: characteristics

transpiration: evaporation of water from a plant

tree cookie: cross section of a tree

unicellular: made up of only one cell

vacuoles: store food, water, and waste for the cell

vascular: having tube-like structures inside the plant to carry food, water, and minerals

vertebrates: animals with backbones

warm-blooded: constant body temperature

woody: hard stems that do not bend easily

xylem: tissue responsible for moving water up from the roots to the other parts of the plant

zoologist: a person who studies animals

Unit One: Teacher Resource Pages

National Science Education Standards Correlation

NSES: (5–6) Strand 3: Characteristics and Interactions of Living Organisms

NSES: (5–6) Strand 7: Scientific Inquiry

NSES: (5–6) Strand 8: Impact of Science, Technology, and Human Activity

Unit One: Overview

- All living things share some common characteristics.
- Scientists have divided the world of living things into five main groups called kingdoms.
- All living things are made up of cells.
- There are two types of cells: eukaryotic and prokaryotic.
- There are three main parts of a cell: nucleus, cell membrane, and cytoplasm.
- Plant and animal cells have many similarities as well as many differences.
- Molecules move in and out of the cell in a process called diffusion.
- Osmosis is a special kind of cell diffusion that occurs with water.
- Cell division is called mitosis.
- Cell reproduction is called meiosis.
- DNA is the blueprint of life.
- Every living thing is a collection of inherited traits.
- Genes are made up of DNA and are located on the chromosomes.
- Plants can be divided into two major groups: vascular or nonvascular.
- Plants reproduce either sexually or asexually.
- Plants that reproduce sexually can be divided into two groups: angiosperms and gymnosperms.
- Vascular plants have three parts: leaves, stems, and roots.

- Flowers have the special job of reproduction for the plant.
- Seeds have three parts: seed coat, embryo, and cotyledon.
- Most seeds are either monocot or dicot.
- The animal kingdom is divided into two groups: vertebrates and invertebrates.
- Invertebrates include sponges, hollow-bodies, worms, mollusks, and arthropods.
- Vertebrates include mammals, reptiles, amphibians, birds, and fish.

Enrichment Activities

Living and Nonliving Collage

Directions: Create a collage or patchwork picture to illustrate living and nonliving things. Divide a sheet of paper in half. On one half, glue pictures of living things. Continue cutting out and gluing pictures until the section is filled. On the other half of the paper, do the same for pictures of nonliving things. Correctly label each side.

Classification

Directions: Divide students into teams. Give each team an assortment of buttons. Students examine the buttons and choose one trait or feature that will allow the group to sort the buttons into groups. After sorting the buttons, each team shares their classification system and compares it to the systems chosen by other teams. Discuss and compare button classification to the way scientists classify living things. (Both are grouped according to similarities.)

Giant Cell Model

Directions: Divide the class into two teams to form giant plant and animal cells. For each team, select several students to form an outside circle to represent the cell membrane. (To construct a plant cell, add an outer circle of students to be the cell wall.) Give one student a paper labeled nucleus. Give remaining students papers labeled with the names of the cell organelles. Students arrange themselves inside the circles. Discuss the functions of the cell organelles, nucleus, cell membrane, and cell wall. Compare the plant and animal cells.

Diffusion

Directions: Select an assortment of balloons and liquid food flavoring: vanilla, maple, banana, and coconut. Using a funnel, add a couple of drops of one flavoring to a balloon. Blow up the balloon and tie the end. Complete the procedure for each of the other food flavorings. After several minutes, pass the balloons around the class. Ask students to smell the balloons. Discuss how the smells of the food flavorings were able to escape the balloons. Discuss and compare this activity to diffusion that occurs in cells. (The balloon and cell membrane have small pores that allow molecules to pass through.)

Mendelian Traits

Directions: Graph the Mendelian Traits of the class. Tally the characteristics and make a pie chart.

How Plants Reproduce

Directions: Plant tulip bulbs, ivy, potato eyes, strawberries, and other plants that demonstrate asexual reproduction. Students observe and record growth.

Classifying Angiosperms and Gymnosperms Activity

Directions: Divide a sheet of drawing paper in half. Label one half angiosperms and the other half gymnosperms. Using magazines and seed catalogs, cut out plant pictures and glue them under the correct headings on the paper.

Photosynthesis Activity

Directions: Place a small piece of wood on a section of lawn. Leave the wood on the grass for two or three days. Remove the wood and note any changes in the grass. Leave the wood off the grass. Observe the area each day. Record any changes in the grass.

Grow a Lawn Activity

Directions: Grow grass seed on a sponge placed in water in a dish. Mow the sponge lawn after the grass grows to 3 inches tall by cutting the grass with scissors. Trim the grass, leaving the lawn one inch tall. Observe what happens to the sponge lawn.

Examining Seeds

Directions: Gather a variety of cones, nuts, and fern spores. Have students examine the items using a magnifying glass and record their observations.

A Diet of Plants

Directions: Students record and graph the parts of plants eaten for a week: roots, flowers, seeds, fruits, and stems.

Decomposers Activity

Directions: Mix sand and topsoil. Fill a glass gallon jar or transparent plastic container $\frac{3}{4}$ full with the mixture. Add 10 to 12 worms to the container. Keep the soil moist, but not wet. Place the container in a cool, dark place. Feed the earthworms a tablespoon a week of fresh or decaying leaves, celery leaves, fruit peelings, or cornmeal. Moisten the food and put a thin layer of fresh soil over it. Throw away any food that becomes moldy or smells bad.

Websites

Cells

"Cells: Mitosis." eMINTS and the Curators of the University of Missouri. University of Missouri. <http://www.biology.arizona.edu/cell_bio/tutorials/cell_cycle/main.html>

Dr. Scott Poethig, Dr. Ingrid Waldron, and Jennifer Doherty. "Using a Microscope to See Different Types of Cells." Department of Biology. University of Pennsylvania. <http://serendip.brynmawr.edu/sci_edu/waldron/microscope.html>

Karen Hagen. "Comparing Prokaryotic and Eukaryotic Cells." University of Alberta. <http://www.biology.ualberta.ca/facilities/multimedia/uploads/cell_biology/provseuk.html>

Mitosis and Meiosis

"Mitosis and Meiosis." University of Alberta. <http://www.biology.ualberta.ca/facilities/multimedia/uploads/genetics/celldivisionMar1.html>

"Comparison of Meiosis and Mitosis." McGraw-Hill Companies, Inc. <http://highered.mcgraw-hill.com/sites/0072437316/student_view0/chapter12/animations.html#>

Osmosis

"Osmosis." Portland State University. <http://edtech.clas.pdx.edu/osmosis_tutorial/>

Genetics

"DNA Detectives." Canadian Museum of Nature. <http://www.nature.ca/genome/03/d/40/03d_40_ee.cfm>

American Museum of Natural History. <http://www.ology.amnh.org/genetics/stufftodo/bracelet_need.html>

"DNA Chain Letter." SuccessLink Inc.<http://www.successlink.org/gti/gti_lesson.asp?lid=2716>

Trees

"Dendrochronology." MSU Museum. Minnesota State University. <http://www.mnsu.edu/emuseum/archaeology/dating/dat_dendro.html>

"Tree Cookie." Idaho Forest Products Commission. <http://www.idahoforests.org/cookie1.htm>

Answers Keys

Plant and Animal Cell Lab (p. 7)

Conclusion

The onion (plant) and cheek (animal) cells both had a nucleus. The plant cells were shaped like boxes and lined up in rows. The cheek cells were round in shape. Drawings will vary.

Plant and Animal Cell Venn Diagram (p. 8)

1. Plant: cell wall, chloroplast
   Animal: no cell wall, no chloroplast
   Both: nucleus, cell membrane, cytoplasm, Golgi bodies, endoplasmic reticulum, mitochondria, ribosomes, vacuole
2. Animals either have a skeleton or an exoskeleton for support. The cell wall is a rigid structure outside the cell membrane that gives the plant support.

Gelatin Cell Model (p. 9)

Plant cell is still in the milk carton.
- carton: cell wall
- nucleus: raisin
- chloroplasts: celery
- cell membrane: bag
- cytoplasm: gelatin

Animal cell is in the bag.
- nucleus: raisin
- cell membrane: bag
- cytoplasm: gelatin

Osmosis Lab (p. 10)

Observation
1. The iodine moved through the pores in the bag and turned the gelatin brown.
2. The perfume moved through the pores of the bag to the water in the jar.

Apply

The bag represents the cell membrane, and the gelatin represents the cytoplasm of a cell. The iodine moves from the water through the pores of the baggie in the same way food and water passes through the cell's membrane into the cytoplasm. The perfume passes from the gelatin, through the bag, and to the water in the way waste products move out of the cell.

Cell Review (p. 11)

Part I
1. b 2. b 3. a 4. c 5. b

Part II
1. nucleus
2. cell membrane
3. cytoplasm

Part III

nucleus: controls all the cell's activities, contains DNA

cell membrane: thin layer that encloses the cell, controls movement of materials into and out of cell, offers shape and protection for the cell

cytoplasm: gel-like material, contains the cell organelles, protein, and nutrients

chloroplast: helps plants make their food; gives plants their green color

cell wall: provides shape and support for the plant cell

DNA Lab (p. 13)

Observation

slimy white strings of DNA from onion

Apply

Answers will vary. Most students will indicate DNA should look the same no matter from what organism it came. All DNA (plant or animal) has the same chemical makeup: phosphate, deoxyribose (sugar), adenine, cytosine, guanine, and thymine.

Mitosis and Meiosis Models (p. 16)

Mitosis is the division of a cell's nucleus to produce a complete new cell. Meiosis is the division of a cell's nucleus to produce gametes or the reproductive cells: sperm cells and egg cells.

Cell Division Review (p. 17)

Part I
1. d 2. e 3. a 4. b 5. c

Part II
1. Interphase   2. Prophase
3. Metaphase   4. Anaphase
5. Telophase

Part III

Answers will vary
1. Every cell inside an organism has the same genetic code or blueprint. DNA is responsible for passing on the code from one generation to the next.
2. Genes are made up of DNA and are located on the chromosomes.

Punnett Square Activity (p. 19)

1.

Bb	Bb
Bb	Bb

a. **Bb**   b. 100% or $\frac{4}{4}$

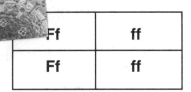

Ff	ff
Ff	ff

a. **Ff, ff**
b. 50% or $\frac{1}{2}$

3.

dd	dd
dd	dd

a. **dd**
b. 0% or $\frac{0}{0}$

Mendelian Traits Activity (p. 20–21)
Answers will vary.

Heredity Review (p. 22)
Part I
1. c 2. a 3. d 4. a 5. b
Part II

Dd	Dd
Dd	Dd

1. **Dd**
2. 100% or $\frac{4}{4}$
Part III
1. Every person is a collection of traits: eye color, hair color, skin color, nose shape, and many others that are inherited from the parents.

Protist Lab (p. 26)
Answers may vary.

Yeast Reproduction Lab (p. 27)
Part I
Answers may vary.
Part II
1. Yeast and water mixture is bubbling.
2. Yeast cells are beginning to bud.

Mold Garden Lab (p. 28)
1. Different colored mold is growing on each cup of soup.
2. food, moisture, warm temperature

Simple Organisms Review (p. 29)
Part I
1. d 2. b 3. a 4. e 5. c
Part II
1. a 2. c 3. d 4. b 5. b
Part III
1. Some monerans are producers. They contain chlorophyll in their cells. Chlorophyll allows a cell to trap the sun's energy. The trapped energy is then used to combine carbon dioxide from the air with water from the environment. When they are combined, the result is food for the cell.
2. Monerans, protists, and fungi are called simple organisms. They are not complicated structures, and they can be easily studied using a microscope.

Vascular Plant Lab (p. 31)
Part I
Celery stalk and leaves have turned red.
Part II
Drawings should show red spots along the cut end of celery piece.
Part III
Vascular. Vascular plants have tube-like structures inside of them that can move food, water, and minerals to the leaves, stems, and other parts of the plant. The food coloring moved through tubes up the stalk of celery to the leaves, so the celery is a vascular plant.

Root Growth Lab (p. 33)
Observation
The sweet potato will sprout in seven to 14 days. First, little white whiskery roots grow under the water. In a week or two, tiny red sprouts appear at the top of the sweet potato. They open into small red-veined green leaves. Next, masses of ivy-like foliage begin to grow at a rapid rate.

Conclusion
The root hairs increase the area available for the absorption of water and other materials the plant needs for growth.

Plant Stem Lab (p. 34)
Observation
One half of the flower is blue and the other half is red.
Conclusion
The stems transport water to the flower and leaf through the xylem.

Sunlight and Photosynthesis Lab (p. 39)
Observation
The leaf turned yellow.
Conclusion
1. The leaf was unable to receive sunlight to make food.
2. The plant would die because plants need sunlight to make their food.

Chlorophyll Lab (p. 40)
Observation
The alcohol turned green.
Conclusion
The chlorophyll the plant uses to make its food was released by the heat and then turned the alcohol green.
Apply
Chlorophyll gives plants their green color. In the fall, plants begin to go dormant and stop making new chlorophyll. The green chlorophyll disappears from the leaves. As the bright green fades away, other colors present in the leaves can be seen.

Plant Respiration Lab (p. 41)
Observation
The leaf will have wilted and turned brown.
Conclusion
There are little openings on the undersides of the leaves called stomata. Carbon dioxide from the air gets into the plant through these

tiny holes. If you plug up these openings, you stop carbon dioxide from getting in, and the leaf can't make food. The leaf dies.

Transpiration in Plants Lab (p. 42)
Observation
The inside of the bag is damp.
Conclusion
During photosynthesis, plants release water through the stomata into the air.

Dissecting a Flower Lab (p. 45)
Observation
Students should see yellow pollen.

Seed Germination Lab (p. 47)
Observation
The seeds in the jars with moist paper towels germinate while the seeds with the dry towels do not.
Conclusion
1. Seeds need water to provide nutrients for growth. The seed absorbs the moisture, and it swells.
2. Seeds need moisture, sunlight, and air to germinate.

Monocot and Dicot Seed Lab (p. 48)
Observation
Drawings should resemble diagram on page 46.
Conclusion
Monocot seeds have one cotyledon, and dicot seeds have two cotyledons.

Monocot and Dicot Plant Activity (p. 49)
1. dicot
2. monocot
3. dicot
4. dicot
5. monocot
6. monocot
7. dicot
8. dicot
9. dicot

Plant Review (p. 52)

Part I

1. d 2. e 3. a 4. c 5. b

Part II

1. d 2. b 3. c 4. c 5. d

Part III

Photosynthesis is the process green plants use to make their food. The leaves containing chlorophyll absorb light energy from the sun. Water and minerals from the soil travel through the roots and stems to the leaves. The water, minerals, carbon dioxide, chlorophyll, and sunlight combine to produce glucose (sugar) and water. Glucose is the usable food for green plants.

Part IV

Angiosperms: flowering plants; seeds surrounded by tissues that become fruit

Gymnosperms: nonflowering plants; produce seeds in cones or spores

Both: reproduce sexually; green plants; stems; leaves; roots

Invertebrate Graphic Organizer (p. 53)

Answers may vary

1. jellyfish
2. round worms
3. flatworms
4. segmented worms
5. arachnids
6. crustaceans
7. centipedes
8. millipedes
9. insects
10. clams
11. starfish

Vertebrates Sorting Activity (p. 56)

Mammals: whale, raccoon, porpoise, armadillo, rabbit, rat, monkey, tiger

Reptiles: snake, alligator, tortoise, turtle

Fish: salmon, trout, shark

Amphibians: frog, salamander,

Birds: bald eagle, cardinal

Animal Kingdom Review (page 57)

Part I

1. mollusks
2. Tentacles
3. mammals
4. Worms
5. Birds
6. cold-blooded
7. warm-blooded
8. Amphibians
9. sponge
10. exoskeleton
11. Arthropods
12. Echinoderms
13. Hollow-bodies
14. Fish
15. reptile
16. Invertebrates

Part II

1. T 2. F 3. F 4. T 5. T

Part III

The exoskeleton is the outer body covering of many invertebrates. It helps protect and support soft tissue. It can be compared to the skeleton of vertebrates.

Name: _____ Date: _____

Ecosystems

Living things can't survive alone. They live in complex communities of many **species** (a group of organisms that can mate and produce offspring), along with nonliving things such as water, soil, and rocks. Scientists study the many different **populations** (all the organisms of the same species) in an **ecosystem** (the combination of living and nonliving elements in a given place) and how they interact.

Relationships in an ecosystem can be complex. Individuals within populations may compete to use the same limited resources: food, water, and space. Only those organisms able to get the resources they need will survive. **Habitat** (where a plant or animal lives in the ecosystem) and **niche** (a special job a plant or animal does in the ecosystem) allow an organism to reduce competition for the things it needs.

Organism	Habitat	Niche
bass	pond	eating minnows
honey bee	field of clover	carrying pollen from one flower to next
earthworm	soil	decomposing dead plants and animals

Predator Prey

Organisms in an ecosystem have special feeding relationships. Some animals are **predators** (kill and eat other animals for energy) and some are **prey** (animals that are killed and eaten for energy). Predator-prey relationships keep an ecosystem balanced by preventing any one population from getting too large.

Predators ⟶ Prey
Lion ⟶ Wildebeest
Great White Shark ⟶ Seal
Coyote ⟶ Rabbit
Fox ⟶ Quail
Hawk ⟶ Mouse

Predator and Prey Activity

Directions: Complete the Predator ⟶ Prey chart using animals you see every day.

Predators ⟶ Prey

_____ ⟶ _____

_____ ⟶ _____

_____ ⟶ _____

_____ ⟶ _____

Name: _____ Date: _____

Symbiosis

Ecosystems are very delicate and must maintain a natural balance. Organisms maintain this natural balance through **symbiosis** (relationships between two organisms). There are three different types of symbiosis.

Types of Symbiosis

Name	Definition	Example
Mutualism	- both organisms benefit	- flower and bee
Commensalism	- one organism benefits - the other is unaffected	- monarch butterfly and milkweed plant
Parasitic	- one organism benefits - the other is harmed	- tick and dog

Symbiosis Graphic Organizer

Directions: Complete the graphic organizer with examples of each type of symbiotic relationship.

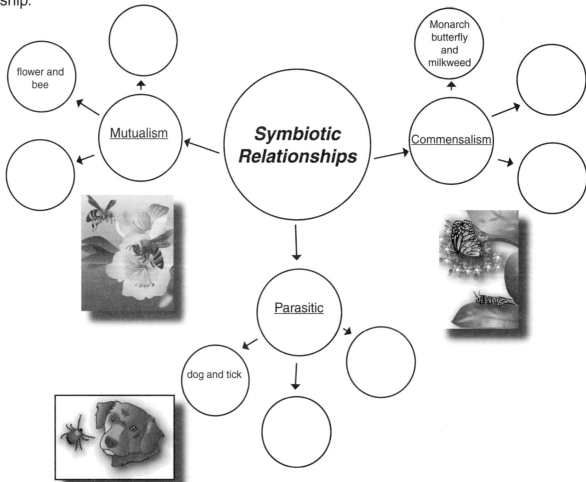

Tracing the Flow of Energy in Ecosystems

All living things need energy. The sun is the main source of energy for most ecosystems. A **food chain** (a diagram of who eats what) is a tool used to trace the energy in food back to the sun. Green plants begin all food chains because they change the sun's energy into food through photosynthesis. Every living thing is part of a food chain. Organisms can be classified as producer, consumer, or decomposer. Each type of organism has an important role to play in the survival of all living organisms.

Name	Definition	Examples
Producers	- organisms that change the sun's energy into food	- green plants
Consumers	- organisms that get energy from eating plants and other animals	- animals
Decomposers	- organisms that get energy from dead or decaying organisms - nutrients from the dead organism become part of the soil - nutrients can then be used by plants	- bacteria - millipede - worms - fungi

Energy Pyramid

All living things constantly consume energy in order to grow and reproduce. The sun provides most of the energy. Green plants and other producers absorb the energy and make food. The food they do not use is stored. The stored energy can be traced through the food chain to other organisms. When animals eat plants and animals, the stored energy in those organisms is passed along to the consumer. Some energy is lost as heat; the rest is used for growth and reproduction. This happens all the way up the food chain. The amount of available energy at each level decreases, limiting the number of organisms that can survive at each level. A kind of **energy pyramid** (a diagram of the loss of useful energy at each level in the food chain) results.

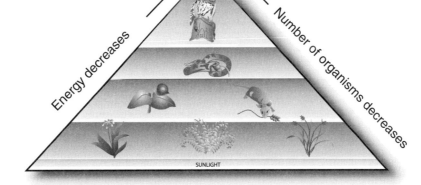

Name: _____ Date: _____

Consumers

All animals are consumers. Each animal has a diet that meets its individual needs for survival. When an animal eats other animals or plants, the stored energy in those organisms is passed along to the consumer. There are three kinds of consumers: herbivores, carnivores, and omnivores.

Name	Definition	Examples
Carnivore	- organism that gets energy from eating other animals	- lions - wolves
Omnivore	- organism that gets energy from eating plants and animals	- humans - bears - raccoons
Herbivore	- organism that gets energy from eating plants	- cows - deer - rabbits

Carnivore, Omnivore, and Herbivore Activity

Directions: Research different animals and their eating habits. Use the information to complete the charts.

Carnivores	Animals They Eat
1.	
2.	
3.	

Omnivores	Plants and Animals They Eat
1.	
2.	
3.	

Herbivores	Plants They Eat
1.	
2.	
3.	

Name: _____ Date: _____

Food Chain Activity

Directions: Color each link in the chain *producer* (green), *consumer* (red), and *decomposer* (brown). Color the sun link yellow. Cut apart the links and glue the ends together to form a forest and an ocean food chain.

	Acorns From An Oak Tree	
	Squirrel	
	Sun	
	Fox	
	Earthworm	

	Emperor Penguin	
	Phytoplankton	
	Killer Whale	
	Squid	
	Krill	
	Sun	
	Zooplankton	

Directions: Create a food chain by filling in the links below. Color each link in the chain *producer* (green), *consumer* (red), and *decomposer* (brown). Color the sun link yellow. Cut apart the links and glue the ends together to form a food chain.

Name: _____   Date: _____

Food Webs

Food chains are not always simple, one-strand chains. They can be very complicated. Producers, consumers, and decomposers interact with each other to make **food webs** (two or more food chains linked together). Food webs represent the flow of energy from one organism to another organism.

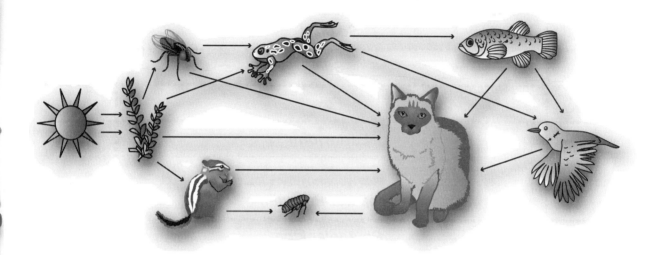

Hanger Food Web Activity

Materials

wire coat hanger   red construction paper   green construction paper
brown paper   yellow construction paper   yarn or string
magazines   colored pencils or markers   drawing paper
twigs (approximately the size of pencils)

Directions

Step 1: Students make a food web on paper. Identify each organism as a producer, consumer, or decomposer.

Step 2: Cut out or draw pictures of the organisms in the food web.

Step 3: Glue the pictures on 3-inch construction paper circles: producers on the green construction paper, the consumers on the red construction paper, and the decomposers on the brown paper.

Step 4: Cut a circle from the yellow construction paper to represent the sun. This circle should fit in the middle section of the hanger.

Step 5: Place a thread through a hole at the top of each circle.

Step 6: Make food chains

Step 7: Connect food chains to make a food web.

Extinct and Endangered Animals

An ecosystem's balance is very fragile. The **extinction** (loss of a species) of one organism in the food chain can damage the whole ecosystem. Many limiting factors can cause the extinction of a species.

Factors that can contribute to extinction:
- habitat destruction
- pollution
- overpopulation
- disease
- climate

Habitat destruction happens as humans expand their claim to territory: land, air, and water. This human expansion causes the animal's territory to decrease, leaving them less room for survival. Habitat destruction not only decreases territory, it also decreases the food supply found in that territory. Organisms need food and space to survive.

Pollution also plays a major part in the extinction of a species. Three types of pollution can affect an animal's habitat. All three types of pollution introduce harmful chemicals and substances into the environment.

Type of Pollution	Examples
Air	- holes in the ozone layer - **smog** (fog that has become mixed and polluted with smoke and automotive emissions) - **acid rain** (precipitation containing harmful chemicals; caused from the gases released during the burning of fossil fuels) - **greenhouse effect** (trapping of gases, mainly carbon dioxide, in the atmosphere causing the earth to heat up)
Water	- rural and suburban pesticide runoff - sewage - chemical dumping - litter
Ground	- litter - trash dumping - chemicals from agriculture and industry

Extinct and Endangered Animals (cont.)

Overpopulation occurs when the number of a species is greater than their environment can sustain. Overpopulation can occur when a species has no natural predator, and their numbers increase faster than the environment can support. The loss of natural predators allows the weaker members of a species to survive, therefore putting more stress on the space, water, and food supply. Overpopulation can cause the spread of diseases that eventually kill an entire species.

The climate can adversely affect a species. **Global warming** (gradual increase in the earth's temperature caused by nature and the burning of fossil fuels) changes temperatures that affect nesting areas, breeding areas, and other important habitats.

Extinction is often a slow process. Species do not just disappear over night. As habitat destruction, pollution, overpopulation, and climate changes take their toll on a species, it becomes **endangered** (any species which is in danger of extinction). If precautions are not taken, the species will become extinct.

Examples of animals that are endangered or extinct (as of December 2007)

Endangered	*Extinct*
- grizzly bear	- Eastern elk
- black-footed ferret	- Carolina parakeet
- ocelot	- blue pike
- Northern sea otter	- Buhler's rat
- blue whale	- Cuban spider monkey
- humpback whale	- Omilteme cottontail
- red wolf	- Steller's sea cow
- Steller sea-lion	- dodo
- short-tailed albatross	- passenger pigeon
- yellow-shouldered blackbird	

Extinction can occur one species at a time or through **mass extinction** (the rapid loss of one or more species). Mass extinction often happens because of drastic environmental changes, such as with the dinosaurs. Mass extinction can also be caused by humans: loss of habitat, pollution, and illegal hunting. Whether a species is destroyed by nature or by humans, the effect on the **biodiversity** (a wide variety of living things in an environment) of the ecosystem can be devastating. Food webs, predator/prey relationships, and the cycling of resources, such as oxygen, carbon dioxide, and nitrogen, are altered, putting the entire ecosystem at risk. Many places have adopted conservation practices in an effort to curb the loss of biodiversity.

Name: _____ Date: _____

Extinction and Endangered Activities

Extinct and Endangered Museum Exhibit

Directions: Research an extinct or endangered species. Topics for research should include habitat, diet, adaptations, and general information about the species. If it is an extinct species, examine which limiting factors caused its extinction. If it is an endangered species, predict why it is on the endangered species list and what measures can be taken to get it taken off the list. Present your research and findings on a display board (the kind commonly used for science fair projects). Display in a classroom museum exhibit on extinct and endangered species.

Protect the Environment Activity

Directions: Write letters to representatives in the United States Congress expressing concerns about habitat destruction and encourage them to support legislation to protect the environment.

Signs of the Times Activity

Directions: Gather newspaper and magazine articles featuring environmental issues locally, nationally, and globally. Create a classroom bulletin board to display the information.

Exxon Valdez Oil Spill

Directions: Research the 1989 *Exxon Valdez* oil spill off the Alaskan coast. What methods were used to clean up the shoreline and animals? What effect did the oil spill have on the marine ecosystem?

Acid Rain Activity

Directions: Scientists believe that acid rain affects how plants grow. Choose two plants. Water one with vinegar and the other with tap water. Place both in a sunny location. Continue to water the plants with the vinegar and tap water over a two-week period. Observe the changes in each plant.

Historical Connection

"Leave it as it is. The ages have been at work on it and man can only mar it."
 – President Theodore Roosevelt
   in a speech at the Grand Canyon in 1903.

Directions: This famous quote sums up the philosophy of today's conservation efforts. Find quotes by other environmentalists. Design a conservation quote bumper sticker.

Name: _____ Date: _____

Oil Spill Simulation Lab

Purpose: Demonstrate how an oil spill can affect a marine ecosystem

Materials Needed

large aluminum baking pan	cotton balls	rocks and gravel
paper towels	water	plastic drinking straws
plastic spoons	motor oil	yarn

Procedure

Step 1: Make an ocean shore line by placing rocks and gravel in one end of the pan.

Step 2: Add enough water to almost cover the rocks.

Step 3: Place several of the cotton balls on the rocks to represent birds and other animals.

Step 4: Add several drops of the motor oil to water to simulate an oil spill.

Step 5: Construct a boom to contain the oil. First, use yarn to try and contain the spill. Next, string plastic straws together and place around the oil.

Step 6: Try different methods to clean up the oil spill: paper towel, plastic spoon, and cotton balls.

Step 7: Remove the boom and allow the oil spill to reach the shoreline.

Observation

1. Which method of cleaning up the oil worked best?

   _____

2. Which method used to contain the spill worked best?

   _____

3. What happened when the oil spill reached the shoreline? Record your observations.

   _____

   _____

   _____

4. Explain why oil spills have such a negative effect on a marine ecosystem.

   _____

   _____

   _____

Name: _____ Date: _____

Predator and Prey Adaptations

Predators will always hunt prey. When the chase is on, each animal has certain adaptations that give it an advantage. Adaptations come in many forms that range from simple coloring to complex body parts.

Predator Adaptations	Prey Adaptations

- good sense of smell
- specialized teeth
- intelligence (larger brain)
- camouflage: color,
  stripes, spots
- larger size
- claws or talons
- specialized tongues
- speed
- venom
	- swivel ears
	- speed
	- antlers or horns
	- larger feet
	- armor or quills
	- stings
	- tusks
	- odor
	- camouflage: color,
	  stripes, spots

Predator and Prey Adaptations Graphic Organizer

Directions: Complete the graphic organizer by filling in the circles with animals that have matching adaptations.

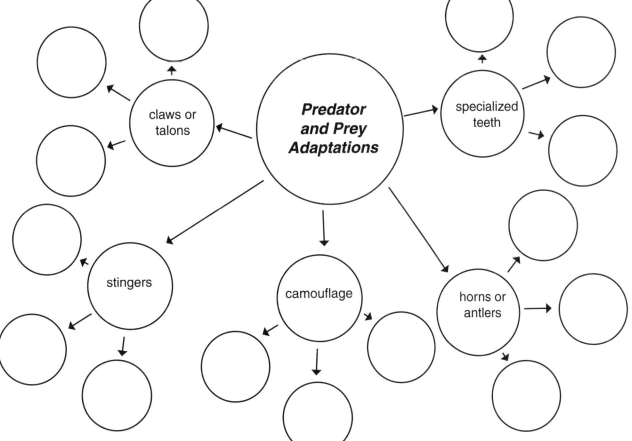

Name: _____ Date: _____

Animal Adaptations Bingo

Directions:

1. Make enough copies of the blank Bingo card for each student.
2. Write the list of animals or adaptations on the board.
3. Students write a different animal or adaptation in each square in any order.
4. Give students approximately 16 markers each (paper clips, sticky notes, etc).
5. Teacher calls out a name of an animal or adaptation.
6. Students put a marker on each square that contains the adaptation or animal called out.
7. Students who get four squares in a row (either across, down, or diagonal) call out "Bingo."
8. Teacher checks the student's answers. If they are correct, the student is the winner. If the answers are incorrect, the game continues until there is a winner.
9. Play as many rounds as desired.

Adaptations:

smell	tusks	stinger	venom	sharp teeth	horns
odor	antlers	claws	color	tongues	spots
stripes	hearing	mimicry	speed	intelligence	

Animals:

skunk	alligator	bee	elephant	bison	copperhead
lion	cheetah	wolf	mosquito	sheep	rattlesnake
deer	badger	frog	coyote	tiger	chameleon
rabbit	piranha	walrus	crocodile		

Name: _____ Date: _____

Ecosystems Review

Part I
Directions: Match the definitions with the correct vocabulary words.

_____ 1. predator
_____ 2. food chain
_____ 3. herbivore
_____ 4. producer
_____ 5. bacteria

a. a diagram of who eats what
b. green plant
c. kills and eats other animals for energy
d. gets energy from eating plants
e. decomposer

Part II
Directions: Write the letter of the correct answer on the line.

_____ 1. A diagram of the loss of useful energy at each step in a food chain is a(n) _____.
   a. energy pyramid   b. food web   c. extinction   d. ecosystem

_____ 2. Where a plant or animals lives in an ecosystem is their _____.
   a. symbiosis   b. species   c. niche   d. habitat

_____ 3. The relationship between a flower and a bee can be _____.
   a. commensalism   b. mutualism   c. parasitism   d. host

_____ 4. The prey of a fox might be a _____.
   a. rabbit   b. deer   c. lion   d. hawk

_____ 5. The niche of a bass might be _____.
   a. eating minnows   b. a pond   c. a river   d. laying eggs

Part III
Directions: Answer the questions in complete sentences.
1. Explain how a symbiotic relationship is different from a predator/prey relationship.

   _____

   _____

   _____

2. What are some ways pollution can contribute to extinction?

   _____

   _____

   _____

Part IV
Directions: Create a food chain diagram on your own paper. Label the producer, consumer, and decomposer.

Ecosystem Cycles

Energy and **matter** (food, water, and air) are continuously being **cycled** (changed and moved) through an ecosystem. All living things constantly consume energy in order to grow and reproduce. The sun provides most of the energy in an ecosystem. The movement of energy through the ecosystem can be traced using a food chain. Organisms need water to stay alive. Water is used to dissolve and transport substance in an organism. Water is moved in a cycle through the ecosystem in the repeated process of evaporation, condensation, and precipitation. Water vapor is also released to the air from the leaves of plants during transpiration. Without **air** (a mixture of gases), most living things would die. Oxygen, carbon dioxide, and nitrogen are three gases organisms must be able to exchange with their ecosystem to survive. The recycling of energy and matter through the **biosphere** (the whole area of the Earth's surface, atmosphere, and sea that is inhabited by living things) keep the ecosystem functioning.

Cycles	Descriptions	Examples
Carbon Dioxide-Oxygen Cycle	- Plants take in carbon dioxide and release oxygen as waste to the environment during photosynthesis. - Most animals take in oxygen and release carbon dioxide as waste to the environment during the process of respiration. - Decomposers break down dead and decaying organisms, releasing carbon dioxide into the environment.	
Nitrogen Cycle	- Decomposers break down dead and decaying organisms, releasing nitrogen. - Some of the nitrogen is absorbed by plant roots and some is released as a gas to the environment.	
Water Cycle	- Water is moved through the ecosystem in the repeated process of evaporation, condensation, and precipitation. - Water is a waste product of plants during the process of photosynthesis. - Water vapor is released to the environment from the leaves of plants during transpiration.	

Name: _____ Date: _____

Water Cycle in a Jar Lab

Purpose: Construct a terrarium in order to observe phases of the water cycle

Materials Needed

jar with lid   water or soda bottle lid
plants   handful of pebbles
potting soil

Procedure

Step 1: Place a handful of pebbles in the bottom of a large jar.
Step 2: Add 2 inches of potting soil.
Step 3: Add plants.
Step 4: Sprinkle water over the soil and plants.
Step 5: Place a small water or soda bottle lid, filled with water, inside the jar.
Step 6: Place the lid on the jar.
Step 7: Place the jar in a warm sunny place.

Observation

After 24 hours, look at the jar terrarium. Record your observations.

_____

_____

_____

Conclusion

1. What role do plants play in the cycling of water in the ecosystem?

_____

_____

_____

2. What phases of the water cycle were demonstrated in the lab?

_____

_____

_____

Apply

What would happen if the cover were removed from the jar?

_____

_____

_____

Biomes

A plant's environment includes several different factors. Weather is one of those factors. Weather includes the amount of sunlight, the range of temperature, and the amount of yearly precipitation. Soil is another factor. The other plants and animals sharing the environment are still another factor. All of the factors together are known as the natural community.

Scientists have divided the world into **biomes** (areas having plants, animals, and climates). Scientists have identified several different land biomes and aquatic biomes.

Biome	Descriptions	Examples of Plants	Examples of Animals
Tundra/ High Mountain	- cold, dry, frozen most of the year	- mosses and lichens, yellow arctic poppies	- caribou, yak, lemmings, arctic hares, snow owls
Forests	- <u>coniferous forests</u>: usually cold winters and cool summers	- cedars, firs, hemlocks, pines, redwoods, spruces, ferns, and mosses	- bears, moose, wolves, ducks, elk
	- <u>deciduous forest</u>: cold winters, warm wet summers	- beeches, birches, chestnuts, elms, hickories, maples, oaks, poplars, walnuts, wildflowers, and shrubs	- deer, raccoons, squirrels, owls, woodpeckers
	- <u>tropical rain forests</u>: warm, wet weather	- mahoganies, teaks, ferns, orchids, and vines	- anteaters, jaguars, boas, toucans, monkeys
Grasslands	- <u>steppes</u>: dry areas	- mostly short grasses	- antelope, bison, wolves, coyotes
	- <u>prairies</u>: dry with some moisture	- tall grasses	- jackrabbits, deer, quail, prairie dogs
	- <u>savannas</u>: dry in winter and wet in summer	- tall stiff grasses, clumps of trees	- giraffes, zebras, jackals, lions
Deserts	- very little rainfall	- cacti, creosote bushes, palm trees, sagebrush, yuccas, wildflowers	- lizards, bobcats, coyotes, rattlesnakes
Aquatic	- <u>freshwater</u>: lakes, rivers, and ponds	- eelgrass, duckweed, cattails	- ducks, frogs, catfish, bass, worms, crayfish
	- <u>salt water</u>: oceans and seas	- kelp, sea lilies, seaweed	- crabs, jellyfish, sharks, whales

Name: _____ Date: _____

Ecological Succession

Living communities change over time. **Ecological succession** (a series of environmental changes that occur in an ecosystem) are the result of the activities of man, other living things, or when natural disasters occur, such as forest fires, floods, climate changes, or volcanic eruptions. These activities may reduce an area to bare soil or rook, but **pioneer organisms** (the first organisms to return to a disrupted area), such as grasses, take root, eventually animals return, and given a sufficient amount of time, new communities form. A **climax community** (stable ecosystem) finally forms that may remain the same for many years.

A Succession Sequence

Ecological Succession Activities

Pond Succession Flip Book

Directions: Over a period of many years, a pond's ecosystem gradually changes and eventually dries out. Research pond ecosystems and succession. Use the research to create a pond succession flipbook. Each page should illustrate and explain one of the four stages in the life of a pond. Label each stage.

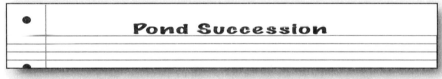

Mount St. Helens Activity

Directions: In May 1980, Mount St. Helens erupted over the course of several hours. Research the natural disaster and the environmental changes that have occurred in the forest ecosystem surrounding the mountain. Using your research, create a three-tab pamphlet to display the information and pictures.

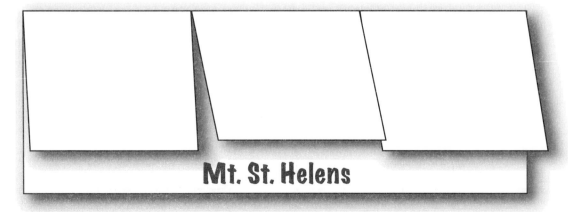

Ecology Triple Play Vocabulary Game

Directions

1. Divide the class into teams. Each team chooses a captain and scorekeeper.
2. Each team receives a copy of the decision cards labeled **True**, **False**, and **Triple Play**.
3. Teacher reads a question to the class. (See *Ecology Triple Play Questions*)
4. Teams decide if the statement is true or false. After a decision has been reached, the captain holds up the **True** or **False** card to show the team's decision.
5. Each team receives five points for every correct answer.

Triple Play Card

Each team may use the **Triple Play** card two times during a game. Along with the decision card, the captain may hold up the triple play card if the team selects this option. If a team decides to use the **Triple Play** card and they answer correctly, the team will receive 15 points. If the team answers incorrectly on a **Triple Play** question, they lose 15 points. Teams should use this tactic on questions they are most confident about answering correctly.

Scoring

Scorekeepers record the points for each question. At the end of the game, the scorekeeper calculates the totals points earned for their team. The team with the highest score wins the game.

Triple Play

True

False

Ecology Triple Play Questions

Questions	**Answer**

1. A food chain is a diagram of who eats what. — **True**

2. Carnivores are organisms that get energy from eating other animals. — **True**

3. Where an animal lives in an ecosystem is its niche. — **False**

    (Where an animal lives in an ecosystem is its habitat.)

4. Decomposers break down dead and decaying organisms. — **True**

5. Pioneer organisms are the first to return to an area after a natural disaster — **True**

    reduces an area to bare soil or rock.

6. Lakes, rivers, ponds, oceans, and seas are examples of tundra biomes. — **False**

    (Lakes, rivers, ponds, oceans, and seas are examples of aquatic biomes.)

7. A biome includes the plants, animals, and climate of an area. — **True**

8. Most of the plants in a broadleaf forest are conifers, such as cedars, firs, and — **False**

    pines. (Most of the plants in a broadleaf forest, such as maples, oaks, and elms,

    are deciduous.)

9. Herbivores are consumers that eat plants and animals. — **False**

    (Herbivores are consumers that eat only plants.)

10. Producers are animals that make their own food using the sun's energy. — **True**

11. Living communities change over time in a process called climax communities. — **False**

    (Living communities change over time in a process called ecological succession.)

12. The living and nonliving things in a given place are called an energy pyramid. — **False**

    (The living and nonliving things in a given place are called an ecosystem.)

13. Predators are animals that are killed and eaten for their energy. — **False**

    (Predators kill and eat other animals for energy.)

14. Air is a mixture of gases. — **True**

15. A special job a plant or animal does in the ecosystem is its niche. — **True**

16. A species is a group of organisms that can mate and produce offspring. — **True**

17. In a parasitic relationship, both organisms benefit. — **False**

    (In a parasitic relationship, one organism benefits and one organism is harmed.)

18. Scientists call all organisms of the same species a population. — **True**

19. Animals that are killed and eaten for their energy are called prey. — **True**

20. Producers are organisms that get energy from eating plants. — **False**

    (Producers are organisms that change the sun's energy into food.)

Ecological Cycles Game

Directions: Cut the cards apart and give one to each student. Students walk around the room and find the other members of their cycle. When students have found their complete cycle, they sit down in order representing the flow of the cycle. Each group explains their cycle to the class.

Carbon Dioxide/ Oxygen Cycle	**Sun** (provides most of the energy in an ecosystem)	**Plant** (takes in carbon dioxide from environment to use during photosynthesis and releases oxygen as waste)
Animal (takes in oxygen from the environment during respiration and releases carbon dioxide as waste)	**Decomposer** (breaks down dead and decaying organisms, releasing carbon dioxide to the environment)	**Nitrogen Cycle**
Decomposer (releases nitrogen from dead plants and animals to the soil)	**Plant** (roots take in nitrogen from soil)	**Animals** (take in nitrogen by eating plants)
Water Cycle	**Sun** (heat from sunlight)	**Evaporation** (liquid water changes into invisible water vapor)
Condensation (clouds form when water vapor cools and turns into tiny liquid water droplets)	**Precipitation** (clouds meet cool air over land and trigger water droplets to fall back to Earth as rain, sleet, or snow)	**Energy Cycle**
Sun (provides most of the energy in an ecosystem)	**Water Plant** (producer)	**Dragonfly** (consumer)
Frog (consumer)	**Snake** (consumer)	**Earthworm** (decomposer)

Name: _____ Date: _____

Ecological Succession and Biomes Review

Part I

Directions: Match the definitions with the correct vocabulary words.

_____ 1. natural community

_____ 2. tundra

_____ 3. ecological succession

_____ 4. climax community

_____ 5. aquatic biomes

a.　areas that remain frozen most of the year

b.　stable community

c.　lakes, rivers, ponds, oceans, and seas

d.　weather, soil, plants, and animals

e.　living communities changing over time

Part II

Directions: Write the letter of the correct answer on the line.

_____ 1. Marine biomes form in the world's _____.
　　　　a. forests　　　b. oceans　　　　　c. deserts　　　　　d. tundra

_____ 2. Trees that annually shed their leaves would be found in a _____.
　　　　a. desert　　　b. coniferous forest　　c. grassland　　　d. deciduous forest

_____ 3. Giraffes, zebras, and lions are examples of animals found in a _____.
　　　　a. forest　　　b. desert　　　　　c. grassland　　　d. tundra

_____ 4. An example of a pioneer plant would be _____.
　　　　a. grass　　　b. coniferous tree　　c. flower　　　　d. deciduous tree

_____ 5. Ecological succession can occur as a result of _____.
　　　　a. hunting　　　b. volcanic action　　c. litter　　　　d. thunderstorms

Part III

Directions: Answer the questions in complete sentences.

1. In 1980, Mount St. Helens erupted, destroying a forest biome. Explain how the process of ecological succession will change the area back to a thriving forest once again.

_____

_____

_____

2. In which biome do you live? Describe the natural community.

_____

_____

_____

3. The sun provides most of the energy for all living things. Explain how this works.

_____

_____

_____

Unit Two: Glossary

acid rain: precipitation containing harmful chemicals; caused from the gases released during the burning of fossil fuels

air: mixture of gases

biodiversity: a wide variety of living things in an environment

biomes: areas having plants, animals, and climates

biosphere: the whole area of the Earth's surface, atmosphere, and sea that is inhabited by living things

carnivore: organism that gets energy from eating other animals

climax community: stable ecosystem

commensalism: one organism benefits and the other is unaffected

consumers: organisms that get energy from eating plants and other animals

cycled: changed and moved

decomposers: organisms that get energy from dead or decaying organisms

ecological succession: a series of environmental changes that occur in an ecosystem

ecosystem: the combination of living and nonliving elements in a given place

endangered: any species that is in danger of extinction

energy pyramid: a diagram of the loss of useful energy at each level in the food chain

extinction: loss of a species

food chain: a diagram of who eats what

food web: two or more food chains linked together

global warming: gradual increase in the earth's temperature caused by nature and the burning of fossil fuels

greenhouse effect: trapping of gases, mainly carbon dioxide, in the atmosphere, causing the earth to heat up

habitat: where a plant or animal lives in the ecosystem

herbivore: organism that gets energy from eating plants

mass extinction: the rapid loss of one or more species

matter: food, water, and air

mutualism: both organisms benefit

niche: a special job a plant or animal does in the ecosystem

omnivores: organisms that get energy from eating plants and animals

parasitism: one organism benefits and the other is harmed

pioneer organisms: the first organisms to return to a disrupted area

population: all the organisms of the same species

predators: animals that kill and eat other animals for energy

prey: animals that are killed and eaten for their energy

producers: organisms that change the sun's energy into food

smog: fog that has become mixed and polluted with smoke and automotive emissions

species: a group of organisms that can mate and produce offspring

symbiosis: one and/or both members of the association benefit from living together

Unit Two: Teacher Resource Pages

National Science Education Standards Correlation

NSES: (5–6) Strand 4: Changes in Ecosystems and Interactions of Organisms With Their Environments

NSES: (5–6) Strand 7: Scientific Inquiry

NSES: Strand 8: Impact of Science, Technology, and Human Activity

Unit Two: Overview

- Organisms live in complex communities.
- Scientists study the many different populations in an ecosystem and how they interact.
- The habitat and niche of an organism reduces competition for the things it needs to survive.
- Predator and prey have special feeding relationships in an ecosystem.
- Organisms in an ecosystem may benefit from symbiotic relationships.
- A food chain is a tool used to trace the flow of energy in an ecosystem.
- Organisms in a food chain can be classified as producer, consumer, or decomposer.
- Carnivores, omnivores, and herbivores are three types of consumers in an ecosystem.

Enrichment Activities

Habitats Activity

Directions: Divide the class into teams. Each team locates a grassy area on the school grounds to observe. They mark the area by placing a hula-hoop on the ground. Teams observe their section for a set period of time. They draw the living and nonliving things and write about any changes they see in their habitat. Compare and contrast the different habitats.

Food Chain

Directions: Write the names of the following organisms on separate index cards: sun, corn, mouse, and fox. Select students to hold the cards in front of the class. Remove one of the organisms from the food chain and discuss the effects the change will have on the community.

Food Web Activity

Directions: Write the names of the following organisms on separate index cards: grain, mouse, grasshopper, snake, hawk, frog, fox, and sun. Give the cards to eight students. Tape the card to the student so that others can see it. Have the students form a circle. Ask each student to tell the name of the organism on the card and indicate if it is a producer, consumer, prey, or predator. Give one student a ball of yarn. The student takes the loose end of the yarn and passes the ball to another. The students continue passing the ball connecting with other students making food chains. Do not cut the yarn until a food web linking together all the food chains has been formed. Discuss how all the organisms are linked and how the elimination of one can have an effect on the entire community of organisms.

Decomposers Activity

Directions: Mix sand and topsoil. Fill a glass gallon jar or transparent plastic container three-fourths full with the mixture. Add 10 to 12 worms to the container. Keep the soil moist but not wet. Place the container in a cool, dark place. Feed the earthworms a tablespoon a week of fresh or decaying leaves, celery leaves, fruit peelings, or cornmeal. Moisten the food and put a thin layer of fresh soil over it. Throw away any food that becomes moldy or smells bad.

Biome Diorama Activity

Directions: Students choose a biome to research. Using the information they find, they construct a diorama illustrating the distinctive kinds of plants and animals as well as the specific climate for the biome.

Desert Garden

Directions: Make a desert garden with cacti. Mix equal parts of potting soil and sand. Put a layer of gravel in the bottom of the dish for good drainage. Spoon the soil and sand mixture into the dish. Plant the cacti in the soil. Add a few tablespoons of water at the base of the cactus plants when the soil is dry. Add pebbles, rocks, or decorative objects to the top of the soil.

Rain Forest Activity

Directions: Students research tropical rain forests. Discover the types of plants and animals living in this type of biome. Using the information, transform one corner of the room into a tropical rain forest. Paint a rain forest mural on butcher paper or newsprint. Tape it to the wall to form the background. Construct life-size plants and animals from butcher paper and add to the corner. Twist brown butcher or craft paper to form long vines. Drape the vines across the corner. Add green leaves and animals. Label and describe each plant and animal placed in the rain forest biome.

Websites
Ecosystems
"Interdependence of Life: Introduction to Eco-systems." Baylor College of Medicine. <http://www.bioedonline.org/slides/slide01.cfm?tk=7>

"Amazon Interactive." Educational Web Adventures. <http://www.eduweb.com/amazon.html>

Food Chain
"Chain Reaction." EcoKids. <http://www.ecokids.ca/pub/eco_info/topics/frogs/chain_reaction/index.cfm>

Food Webs
"Fun With Food Webs." Harcourt School Publishers. <http://www.harcourtschool.com/activity/food/food_menu.html>

Endangered and Extinct Animals
"Finalist - 2000 ThinkQuest USA." ThinkQuest. <http://www.thinkquest.org/library/cat_show.html?cat_id=47>

Answer Keys
Predator and Prey Activity (p. 69)
Answers may vary.

Symbiosis Graphic Organizer (p. 70)
Answers may vary.

Carnivore, Omnivore, and Herbivore Activity (p. 72)
Answers may vary.

Food Chain Activity (p. 73)
- sun, acorn from an oak tree, squirrel, fox, earthworm
- sun, phytoplankton, krill, squid, emperor penguin, killer whale, and zooplankton
- Answers may vary.

Hanger Food Web Activity (p. 74)
Answers may vary.

Oil Spill Simulation Lab (p. 78)
Observation
1. Answers may vary.
2. Answers may vary.
3. The oil coated everything on the shoreline.
4. Oil spills are difficult to contain and clean up on shorelines and marine life.

Predator and Prey Adaptations Graphic Organizer (p. 79)
Answers may vary.

Ecosystems Review (p. 81)
Part I
1. c 2. a 3. d 4. b 5. e
Part II
1. a 2. d 3. b 4. a 5. a
Part III
1. Predators hunt and kill their prey for food energy. Symbiotic relationships depend on both organisms remaining alive.
2. Pollution can poison the air or water an animal needs to live. Answers will vary.
Part IV
Food chains will vary.

Water Cycle in a Jar Lab (p. 83)
Observation
Drops of water formed on the lid of the jar. They became heavy and dropped down to the plants and soil.
Conclusion
1. Plants absorb water from the soil and return it to the atmosphere through transpiration.
2. The sun heats water. When it evaporates, it condenses on the jar and precipitates back to the plants and soil.
Apply
When the sun heats the water and it evaporates, it would leave the jar. The soil would dry out, and the plants would die.

Ecological Succession and Biomes Review (p. 89)
Part I
1. d 2. a 3. e 4. b 5. c
Part II
1. b 2. d 3. c 4. a 5. b

Part III
1. Pioneer organisms, such as grasses, will return, eventually animals return, and given a sufficient amount of time, a new community will form. Finally, a stable community of plants and animals will remain with little change for many years.
2. Answers will vary.
3. Green plants and other producers absorb the sun's energy to make food. Producers begin every food chain. All living things either eat producers or eat the animals that eat the producers.

Additional Resources

Printed

An Introduction to Life, Earth, and Physical Science. Glencoe/McGraw-Hill, 1999.

Cohen, Joy, and Eve Pranis. *GrowLab: Activities for Growing Minds.* National Gardening Association, 1995.

Haven, Kendall and Donna Clark. *100 Most Popular Scientists for Young Adults: Biographical Sketches and Professional Paths.* Libraries Unlimited, Inc., 1999.

Raham, Gary. *Science Tutor: Life Science.* Mark Twain Media, Inc./Carson-Dellosa Publishing Company, Inc., 2005.

Recycle/Reuse. Regents of University of California, 1990.

Routh, Debbie. *Learning About Cells.* Mark Twain Media, Inc./Carson-Dellosa Publishing Company, Inc., 2006.

Routh, Debbie. *Learning About DNA.* Mark Twain Media, Inc./Carson-Dellosa Publishing Company, Inc., 2003.

Sciencesaurus: A Student Handbook. Houghton Mifflin, 2002.

Ward, Barbara and Pat Ward. *Microorganisms.* Mark Twain Media, Inc./Carson-Dellosa Publishing Company, Inc., 1998.

Ward, Barbara and Pat Ward. *Plants: A Science Activity Book.* Mark Twain Media, Inc./Carson-Dellosa Publishing Company, Inc., 1998.

Online

The Biology Corner. <http://www.biologycorner.com/worksheets.php>

"Jell-o® 3-D Animal Cell Craft." Enchanted Learning.com. 2004-2007. <http://www.enchantedlearning.com/subjects/animals/cell/jello/>

"What Do Plants Need To Grow?" Primary Resources. <http://www.primaryresources.co.uk/online/powerpoint/plants.ppt>

"Endangered Species Thrive (In Cyberspace)." Educations World. <http://www.education-world.com/a_curr/curr133.shtml>

"Interdependence of Life: Introduction to Ecosystems." Baylor College of Medicine. <http://www.bioedonline.org/slides/slide01.cfm?tk=7>